15 SECRETS

THE TAXMAN DOESN'T WANT YOU TO KNOW

Plus 10 Bonus Tax Tips

Dwayne Daku

The 15 Secrets The Taxman Doesn't Want You To Know!

by Dwayne Daku

Copyright 2008 Eagle Publishing
First published in 2008
Published by Eagle Publishing
Nassau, The Bahamas

Library and Archives Canada Cataloguing in Publication

Daku, Dwayne, 1947 -

The 15 secrets the taxman doesn't want you to know : plus 10 bonus tax tips / Dwayne Daku.

ISBN 978-1-897010-55-6

1. Income tax–Law and legislation–Canada–Popular works.
2. Tax planning–Canada–Popular works. I. Title.
II. Title: Fifteen secrets the taxman doesn't want you to know.

KE5682.D33 2008   343.7105'2   C2008-907276-6

Artwork by Daniel Giesbrecht
Cover Design by Brian Danchuk,
Brian Danchuk Design, Regina, Saskatchewan
Page formatting by Iona Glabus

Printed and Produced in Canada by:
Centax Books, a division of PrintWest Communications Ltd.
Publishing Director – Dan Marce
Publishing Coordinator – Iona Glabus
1150 Eighth Avenue, Regina, Saskatchewan, Canada S4R 1C9
(306) 525-2304   FAX: (306) 757-2439
E-mail: centax@printwest.com   www.centaxbooks.com

TABLE OF CONTENTS

Acknowledgements

Marlene Daku
Proofing and editing

Daniel Giesbrecht
Illustrations

Ruth
Belief that it could be done

Dan Marce
Ideas and suggestions on how it could be done

Introduction

As you read this book you will probably say to yourself, "these are not really secrets" or "I have read similar books". However, we ask you the question, have you implemented what you know? The purpose of this book is to prompt a change in the way you are handling your financial situation; and if that happens, then we have accomplished what we set out to accomplish with this book. These are not big secrets, but we are willing to bet that if you implement even one of them you will save yourself considerably more tax than the amount you paid for this book. Does that not make it worth its price? Besides, they say that most people retain only 10% of what they read or hear the first time, so a repeat of information serves to reinforce it in your mind. In addition, no doubt many things have changed in your life since you read other books on this subject. So this is a reminder to review your financial situation and make the necessary changes. Even after reading and acting on the concepts in this book, we suggest that you read it at least once a year as a reminder that your life is changing and your financial plans need updating.

When I tell people that I am writing a book with the title, *The 15 Secrets The Taxman Doesn't Want You To Know!*, after their initial interest I often get the comment, directly or implied, that "it is not right to tell people how to reduce their taxes, for everyone should pay their fair share". The implication of course being that by giving this information on how to use the tax laws, somehow we are urging people not to carry their weight, and that what we are suggesting is at the least unfair, if not illegal. The response we give to that is, we are not encouraging the breaking of laws, in fact far from it. We are simply saying that the average taxpayer needs to be able to properly use the tax system to keep money that is legitimately theirs. Besides, we believe the average taxpayer can more effectively use the money they might save in reduced taxes, than what the government does with it. Then I ask the question "Do you like the way the government is spending YOUR money?" That usually ends the conversation quite quickly and has them asking where they can get a copy of this book.

When we first planned and began to write this book, we struggled with what name to put on the cover. For most of its life the Canadian government tax department was known as Revenue Canada, but a few years ago they changed their name to Canada Customs and Revenue Agency. However that did not last very long and most recently they have changed their name to Canada Revenue Agency. In the criminal world one changes their name or uses another, whenever they feel that people are getting wise to what they are doing, or they are seeking to cover up and escape past actions. Why do we get the feeling that there is little difference here? So throughout the book we are using the name by which the federal tax department is most commonly known, Revenue Canada.

> **" Ninety percent of the politicians give the other ten percent a bad reputation."**
>
> - Henry Kissinger

" The politicians don't just want your money. They want your soul. They want you to be worn down by taxes until you are dependent and helpless. When you subsidize poverty and failure, you get more of both. "

- James Dale Davidson

" If Patrick Henry thought that taxation without representation was bad, he should see how bad it is with representation."

- Old Farmers Almanac

Our Tax Problem is a "Want" Problem

It seems that every political party before they are elected, promises in some way to make changes to the tax system but when they get into power, they never do. There are token "bones" thrown to the electorate but never anything substantial, and most often the only change is an increase of the over all tax bill.

We believe that the basic problem in our tax system is a philosophical one, which as a result becomes a logistical one. The major problem as we see it is "want". The political parties offer all kinds of things in their effort to encourage us to elect them. They "want" power because they believe they know what is best for us. If you don't believe that, all you have to do is take a close look at a political party leadership race and see who wants power and how badly. Then, once this politician does get elected, their primary concern becomes what must they do to get re-elected. As the chapter title says, the problem is a "want" problem. Everybody wants something.

We, the electorate are not much different. Which party do we vote in? The one that promises us the most with the least amount of pain. We especially want to vote in the group of people who promise to give us all kinds of benefits while having the "other guy" pay for them. Unfortunately, this whole attitude causes major problems both in governing and paying for government.

So, the tax problem is really a "want" problem. We all want something (usually a lot of things) and the result is that someone needs to pay for these "wants", so taxes keep going up. In fact, they go up at a frightening rate. In 2008, the Fraser Institute, a Canadian Research Company based in Vancouver, tabulated that the tax bill for the average Canadian has increased from 33.5% of their income in 1961 to 45.4% in 2007. Of course incomes have increased over the same period of time, going from an average of $5,000 per year to $66,496 per year. The frightening thing is that in that same period of time, the government tax grab went from $1,675 in total taxes per average taxpayer, to $30,213. An increase of 1,700%! As already stated, in 1961 the government took only 33.5% of the average income, and the average family at that time spent 56.5% of their income for housing, clothing and food. By 1981, the average Canadian was able to increase his total income so that his housing, clothing and food costs were only 40.8% of his income. However, rather than having extra money to put into his jeans, the government now took 40.5%. By 2007 real income had increased and living costs had been reduced to the point where the average Canadian only had to use 35.6% of his income to cover his necessities, but the government was taking 44.9%. In summary, during that period of time the cost of clothing increased by 455%, food by 505%, housing by 1063%, but taxes by 1700%. The Fraser Institute concludes that taxes have been the single biggest expense to Canadians in the last 46 years. Something is dreadfully wrong with the picture when the government is taking more of your money than you are needing to live.

If ever-increasing taxes do not provide enough cash for the government to fund their programs, they resort to borrowing to cover their expenditures. In fact the problem has become so bad, that as of May 2008 our combined debt for all levels of government was $2.3 trillion, up from $533 billion in 1990/1991. That means every taxpayer owes $150,211 (or $75,942 per Canadian citizen) in government debt when we factor in the debt in ALL levels of the economy: federal, provincial, and local. The most disturbing part of these numbers is that they do not include the unfunded liabilities for our social programs. These combined total over $1.3 trillion.

Who is going to make up the shortfall to cover the Canada pension that has been promised to you when you retire? When the Canada Pension Plan was first implemented, projections indicated that there would be enough taxpayers available to fund the rather conservative payments that would be made. However since then, payments have increased dramatically and the birth and immigration rate has gone down to the point that it is now estimated that by 2040, 26.5% of the population will be drawing pensions. I repeat, who is going to pay for this, unless the government begins setting aside major funds now, if it is not already too late?

To give you an example how bad this debt really is; if the Quebec government taxed at 100% all income generated in the province, it would take 2.5 years to pay off all debt and fund all the obligations they currently have.

Are our demands that high? Maybe, but I suggest that perhaps the biggest problem is the way the government is spending your money. In a recent report the Auditor General stated that our government's delivery of general services (when compared to other countries), showed that about 25% of the cost for those services was "waste", due to inefficiency and the waste of material. In other words if the various departments were managing their operations as they should, the services they provide could cost the taxpayer 25% less than what they do now. Your overall tax bill could be 25% less and you would still get the same "quality" of service.

What are they doing with your money? The answer to that question is very frightening. There are far too many illustrations but we want to bring a few to your attention.

Did you know that:

- the top man at Revenue Canada brags that he has an annual budget of over $4 billion and over 46,000 people on staff, to make sure you pay the government the money they believe you owe?

- the top taxman at Revenue Canada spent $40,000 of your money for a new washroom in his office suite in 2007? (An internal government memo April 10, 2007 shows that someone questioned this expense for his washroom but a further memo stated "that in the absence of "clear standards" for the offices of senior officials, the washroom might be considered a "special facility.") At $40,000 plus it must be really "special"!

- Revenue Canada receives oversight from a board of 15 members and that these members in 2007 received over $407,000 EACH, in fees and retainers for their **part-time** position?

- these board members meet about 5 times a year for retreats & business and that just one of these retreats in September of 2006 cost you/us an additional $91,000 for 3 days (above their regular compensation)?

- in the year 2005-06, the top 16 Revenue Canada commissioners and their 6 deputy assistants received a total of $3.3 million dollars in salaries?

This is the same agency that will grind and threaten you for the $100 you did not accurately declare on your 5 year old tax return (that they are just now auditing) and in addition to that $100, they will also be assessing you interest and penalties for that 5 year period of time.

➤ To add insult to injury, the Canadian Press reporter, Dean Beeby reported that as of February 2008, CRA had issued pay cheques totalling at least $3 million dollars to people who no longer work for the CRA. There are more details available about this, but in most cases it was over payment to people who had left its employ but continued to get a pay cheque. Apparently now CRA is looking into how they can write that off, for they believe there is no hope of ever collecting. This is the organization that is hassling you for the few dollars they claim you owe them.

Did you know that:

➤ if the Kyoto Protocol is implemented as agreed to, it is estimated that it will cost the average Canadian $3,500 each over the next 5 years in extra taxes and reduced income?

➤ the Auditor General says that there are 2.4 million more SINs (Social Insurance Numbers) than Canadians, but they cannot put their finger on exactly who these people are and how much they are siphoning (scamming) the system for? Estimates are between $377 million and $2.4 billion. Revenue Canada says there is just no way that these numbers can be accurately tracked down. Yet they can track down the $100 they say you owe because of some "incorrect" deduction you made.

➤ in 2002 the Department of National Defense completed the development of a special custom satellite communications system at a cost of $174 million but then concluded that the commercial system that they were currently using was better and took less staff? Even if they now decided to use the new system, it would take an additional $15 million to bring it up to current standards. As a result it is in storage while our soldiers try to do their duty with equipment that is considered to be below standard because there wasn't "enough funding".

➢ in an attempt to reduce the cost of embassy properties, Foreign Affairs sold one ambassadorial residence for $12 million and then leased space for $350,000 plus $300,000 in renovations? It sounds like a step in the right direction. However, the ambassador refused to vacate the "sold" residence and the project was cancelled, and I imagine we are probably still paying for a lease on that new property. I think the ambassador, an unelected official, needs to be reminded who he is really working for and who pays the bills.

➢ between 1982 and 2005 the Federal Government provided $7,140,796 in "repayable funding", in other words "loans", to an assortment of 61 organizations. "Needy" organizations with names like Department of Industry Act – Sec. 13 & 14, St. Lawrence River Environmental Technology Development Program, and Hydrogen Early Adopters Program? A few of them have completed their repayment commitment but so far only 17.6% of that amount loaned has been repaid, and the Auditor General feels there is little hope of collecting the balance. Who loans out your money and by what criteria? If this were any other loans company, the person in charge would be long gone.

➢ in 2004, you the taxpayer, provided businesses with $19 billion dollars in subsidies? That was $1,295 for every taxpayer that year and the top recipients of these subsidies were "needy" companies like Pratt & Whitney, General Motors Canada, Magna Corporation, a Mont Tremblant ski resort, and Alcan, to name only a few. These were not loans! No repayment was required! They were outright subsidies (gifts). We realize that the "purpose" behind these subsidies is supposed to be to stimulate the economy and provide more jobs, but there are usually no measurable results. So we have no idea what we got for our money.

➢ the city of Edmonton, in their effort to promote Edmonton to people in Washington DC, on Canada Day hired actors from Washington to hand out yo-yos with Edmonton's logo and website address on it? The cost – $30,000. I wonder how many people visited Edmonton because of it? Are you willing to take a guess?

➢ each year the Tax Payers Association gives out the Teddies, which are awards given for people either in government or in the public arena who have blatantly misused public funds? They were named after a former senior public servant, who according to the Office of the Minister of Labour, was terminated in 1999 "for expenses incurred by him … incompatible with his position as Chairman of Canada Labour Relations Board". In other words he wasted a lot of your money.

In 2007, the Federal winner was a Canadian senator, in the "Achievement in Use of Extras" category. We are not sure how he votes in the senate, or if he votes, or how often he even shows up, but we know he had a government staff member cut down the trees on his neighbour's property in western Quebec. As a result of the investigation into the use of his staff member to cut down the trees, he has been charged with fraud and in addition has been ordered to pay back $23,500 in misappropriated travel. He has also been charged with breach of trust and obstruction of justice. Even after the sponsorship scandal the Liberals feel that he is not someone they want in their caucus and they have also given him the boot.

These actions and others on the part of senators revisits the question as to whether the senate is a good expenditure of your money?

Did you know that (this one bothers me the most):

> ➤ with the price of gasoline fluctuating as high as $1.30 per litre, 34 to 48 cents of that (depending on the province) is tax? Built into that $1.30 are several earlier federal taxes, and then there is the tax the provinces charge, and finally the Feds put the GST on top of all the other taxes. A tax on tax and more tax on taxes. For every 10 cents per litre increase at the pump, Ottawa collects an additional 100 million dollars in GST annually. And you wonder why there is no action on the part of politicians to address the growing cost of fuel. What would you do to have an almost limitless stream of cash that you could squander foolishly and without explanation? If a "carbon tax plan" of any kind gets implemented, these numbers will seem like peanuts compared to what we will then have to pay.

We wish we could provide an easy solution to the way the government wastes your money, but that can only be done by those we elect and they seem unable or unwilling to deal with it. We must put more pressure on our elected officials by joining groups who will speak for us, such as the Canadian Taxpayers Association. (**www.taxpayer.com**)

It is this blatant abuse of our money that causes us to write a book to assist you to legally keep tax dollars that you do not owe, so that Revenue Canada and the government of Canada cannot waste them. We believe that you will more wisely use your money than the government ever will.

We must share one news event before closing this chapter. In 2006, Jack Kundert was taken to court in Windsor, ON, by Revenue Canada because he "refused" to pay his taxes. Revenue Canada claimed that he owed $350,000 in taxes, stating that between 1993 and 1998 he had earned 1.5 million dollars, but on his tax return he wrote "zero income". The charge was "tax evasion" but Jack declared he was simply "protesting" the tax system because it had been brought in as a temporary measure and therefore was unconstitutional. Besides he said, revealing his earnings to the government would be like "sitting down with thieves" and telling them where his valuables were kept.

The jury of his peers apparently agreed that there was no criminal intent and found him not guilty of "tax evasion". We are sure we have not heard the end of this story, for Revenue Canada is relentless in what they think is theirs and does not give up easily, but it does show what most people think of Revenue Canada.

In spite of claims by the government to overhaul the tax system, we feel that people are still in need of tips and direction as to how they can reduce their tax obligations, legally and fairly. Because of the abuses stated above, in this book we seek to give advice on how to effectively reduce your taxes legally, while at the same time the government tries to find ways to take more money from you to waste on their wild ideas and profligate spending.

> "Don't worry about people stealing your ideas. If your ideas are any good, you'll have to ram them down people's throats."
>
> Howard Aiken, American scientist, 1900-1973

A Taxing Solution

> " The hardest thing in the world to understand is income tax."
>
> - Albert Einstein

In a survey, when given a choice, 52% of taxpayers said they would prefer a trip to their dentist over preparing their tax return themselves. Why is this? Because the whole Income Tax Act has grown so huge and complicated that only specially trained professionals can sort out what you can claim and apply to your situation. In 1917 there were 11 pages comprising the Canadian Tax Code, which was to be a temporary act of parliament to help fund the First World War. Today there are 2,226 pages and growing. Estimates indicate that the cost of having their taxes prepared, costs the average taxpayer somewhere between $585 and $955 for every person in the country. This is a direct out of your pocket expense and does not include one cent of what the Revenue Canada department is costing us to collect the taxes. This same estimate calculates that our complicated tax system devours somewhere around $30 billion annually in the preparation of tax returns and the collection of taxes. Don't you feel that this money could be better spent in another way? We sure do!

The statistics from the year 2007 shows that 30% of the families in Canada earned 60% of the income. However to be included in that top 30%, their total income had to exceed $81,501. The amount of money that they earned seems a little unfair until you discover that they also paid 66% of all taxes. On the opposite end, the bottom 30% earned 8.4% of the income but paid only 4.8 % of the tax.

Before we share the secrets that will be presented later in this book, there is one area where we feel a simple solution must be proposed. That is in the way income tax is collected. What if, instead of filling out elaborate forms and providing receipts and forms, you could take about 15 minutes early in April and fill out a form about the size of a postcard, which would complete your tax return? This can and is being done in many countries today. What is it? The term generally used is **FLAT TAX**.

Briefly, this is how it works. When it is time to complete your tax return you fill in the amount that is your total income. You can get that in the same way you do now. Then you subtract the basic personal exemption and on that balance everyone pays the same rate of tax, probably somewhere around 15%. You have just calculated the tax you owe! Too simple? Does it look like someone may get away without "paying their fair share"? Let's look at some possible scenarios.

A. You earn $20,000 per year. The basic personal exemption is $19,500. Your taxable income therefore is $500 and at a 15% flat tax rate, your income tax would be $75.

B. You earn $63,000 per year (the current Canadian average). Again the personal exemption of $19,500 applies. Your taxable income is $ 43,500 and at 15% your tax comes to $6525.

C. Your income is $200,000 per year. Again we subtract the personal exemption of $19,500. Your taxable income is $180,500 and at 15% your tax comes to $27,075.

Does this look fair to you? It does to me, and more than that, it is **simple**. Probably too simple for the politicians for they will always find some way to complicate it, and allow loop holes for some one to squeeze through and not pay their fair share. Maybe it sounds too simple. You know the saying, "if it sounds too good to be true it must be". But this adage does not apply in this case. It does work, and works very well in a number of countries, like Hong Kong.

Hong Kong is a country that has been Number 1 on the list of "Economically Free" countries for many years (Canada is Number 5 on that list). It has had this flat tax in effect since 1947. Instead of 66,000 pages of tax codes and regulations as the US does, Hong Kong has 200 pages. The result is that it has a small government bureaucracy and yet one of the highest per capita incomes in Asia. Even the Chinese government on the mainland knows better than to tamper with this successful model of financial power.

With a flat tax there would no longer be the penalty of increasing tax rates as you earn more, but of course there would still be increased taxes to remit because you earned more. With a flat tax people would be able to keep more of their hard earned money that would result from entrepreneurship, saving, and investing. We realize that if this system were adopted there would be no sales for this book, and accountants and tax preparers would have their work load dramatically reduced, but we are willing to pay that price to simplify the tax system. The most exciting thing about a **FLAT TAX** is that there would be no need for Revenue Canada and their arrogant attitude and waste. Let's start talking about it and get in touch with our politicians to look seriously at the matter.

A study of the countries where such a **FLAT TAX** has been implemented, shows that in every case the rate came down from that initially set, because there were no longer loopholes for crafty tax lawyers to help their wealthy clients escape through and
everyone paid their fair share!

1 Working Your Plan

> " If you don't know where you are going, you may wind up someplace else."
>
> - Yogi Berra

Can you imagine this scenario – you decide to take a holiday and phone up your travel agent and tell them that you "want to take a trip", but that is all you say. No doubt there would be a pause before the telephone conversation resumed and then the agent would begin to ask you a number of questions. Questions such as where do you want to go? When do you plan to leave and return? How much money do you plan to spend? And so on. We realize that such a telephone call is ridiculous, for no one would begin a telephone call to their travel agent in that way. Unfortunately, that is the way many people plan their financial lives ... if they plan at all. They want a good retirement but have no plan as to what it will be like and how they will get it.

A commonly used adage says, "**Plan your work and then work your plan**". Therefore in this book we are going to include a brief chapter on goal setting and developing a plan. If you do not have goals you are going to accomplish exactly what you have set out to accomplish. Someone once said that one definition of insanity is "**doing the exact same thing over and over again, but expecting a different result each time**". There are any number of books on goal setting and most are very good, so we are not going to re-invent the wheel, but simply re-emphasize that when it comes to your financial situation you must have definite goals or you are going to end up like Yogi Berra said in the opening quote.

Let's do some very preliminary goal setting just to get you thinking in that direction. On a separate piece of paper simply brain storm for a few minutes by writing down the answers to the following general questions.

1. Where do you want to be and what do you want to be doing when you retire? This may not seem important to you right now, especially if you are under 40 years of age, but the retirement years sneak up very quickly and suddenly you are facing them head on. Also, make sure that your goals are something you really want, not just something that sounds good.

2. What amount of income will you need to do what you want to do when you retire? Because one cannot accurately account for inflation in all of these projections, just use today's dollars to give you a rough idea of what it would take if you made that move today.

3. How much are you setting aside right now to accomplish that goal? The earlier you start the easier it is and the less you will need to contribute in total. Consider these options if you want to have 1 million dollars in investments at age 65, using a 10% interest rate:

   a. If your parents started your retirement fund when you were born, they/you will only have to contribute $15.50 per month to reach that $1 million goal. Your total actual contributions will be just over $12,090.

b. If you begin to save when you are 20 years of age your contributions will need to be $96.00 per month and you will end up contributing nearly $51,840.

c. If you don't start toward your goal until you are 40 you will need to contribute $695.00 per month and your total contributions will be nearly $208,500.

d. If your parents started the plan when you were born and put away only $18.15 per month for the first 20 years you would still reach your goal and the total contributions would be $4,356.

So, Earlier is Better, but starting any time is better than not starting at all.

> **" Before we can go forward, we need to know where we are now."**
> — Rules of Wealth # 19

If you feel that you do not have surplus funds now to begin to save, take a look at an accurate record of where you are currently spending your money. We mean accurately and detailed. Most people know the costs of their major expenses but forget about the little items that are eating away what they could be saving. Meals out, gourmet coffees, or the like. Our suggestion is that for a period of not less than three months, keep track of every penny you spend (even that package of gum). Then at the end of that period, tally it all up and you will be surprised as to where you could find some money to set aside each month.

4. The crucial part of putting together this plan is that you have definite details, such as goal dates, precise dollar amounts, and specifics in your goals. You then have a measuring stick to evaluate your position and see what progress you are making.

So the 4 basic rules of good **goal setting** are:

➢   must be clear and specific.
➢   must contain a time element.
➢   must be consistent.
➢   must be achievable.

This could be an example of the statement for one specific goal. In 5 years we will be 35 years of age, we will have paid off 50% of our home mortgage, have an after tax income of $60,000, with investments totaling $50,000 in value. In 10 years we will be 40 years of age and will have paid off 75% of our home mortgage, have an after tax income of $80,000, with investments totaling $80,000 in value. When we retire our mortgage will be paid in full; all vehicles paid in full; and we will have investments that will pay a before tax income of $90,000; so that we can travel to a warmer destination for a period of not less than eight weeks each year. To do this we will need investments of at least $1 million.

As you can see these goals are very specific and precise. Now that you have yours, what needs to be done next is to have them broken down by the year and for the first 5 years by each month.

> " Failure isn't in not reaching your goal, but in having no goal to reach."
> — Benjamin Mays

This will give definite targets and numbers by which you can measure your progress.

View your financial plan as a Global Positioning System (GPS). You enter into the program where you are now and where you want to end up. Then the rest of the plan is directed by these two pieces of information. With a GPS you can tweak it a bit; by giving the instructions that you want to take a scenic route, or some place you may want to stop on the way. Those of you who have driven with a GPS know if you miss a turn or head in the wrong direction, the GPS immediately tells you of your error and what can be done to correct it. Look at your financial plan as if it is your GPS. Following it closely will get you to your destination but there **IS** room to make adjustments and changes as you go.

When it comes to goal setting you cannot be too specific, but you must change your **mind set** to put it all together. A friend of mine once said to me, "**If you think the way you've always thought, you will continue to get what you've always got.**" I don't know if that originated with him or if he borrowed it from somewhere else, so I cannot give precise credit, but it is very true. Begin to think differently today, and put your plan on paper. It can be adjusted as you go, but at least you will know where you are going.

> " **A man who removes mountains begins by carrying away small stones."**
> - William Faulkner

One small "stone" could be to simply begin to save $1.00 per day. This seems like a very small stone but over a period of time it could become of great value. Look at the following table and see what one little "stone" and compound interest can amount to over the years. Then visualize what happens if you increase it to $2.00 or perhaps $5.00 per day.

# of Years	Total Contributed	Total Value at Various Interest Rates		
		5%	7.50%	10%
5	1825	$2,118	$2,279	$2,451
10	3650	$4,820	$5,551	$6,399
25	9125	$18,291	$26,673	$39,486
50	18250	$80,233	$189,333	$467,309
65	23725	$175,068	$570,460	$1,964,823

Now go, buy or borrow a few good books on goal setting and get started. The Resources on page 128, offer some suggestions on where to begin.

" Don't be pushed by your problems. Be led by your Dreams."

- Annonymous

> " I cannot teach anybody anything,
> I can only make them think."
>
> - Socrates

> "An obstinate man does not hold opinions, they
> hold him."
>
> Alexander Pope, 1688-1744

2 **Payroll Withholding**

Although most people do not look forward to tax time, there are some people who actually want to get their taxes done as quickly as possible. Why? Because they usually have a sizeable tax refund coming and they want to know how much it is and look forward to spending it. I don't believe you are like that, for if you were, you probably would not be reading this book.

Stats Can indicates that in 2005 about 24 million tax returns were filed and of those nearly 60% were owed a refund averaging about $1,000. Do the math – 14.16 million returns times $1,000 means that for at least a portion of the year Revenue Canada had money in their possession that was not rightfully theirs. In any other situation we would label that person a thief, but because these taxpayers actually give permission for this, Revenue Canada can get away with it.

This secret is the one that Revenue Canada most wants to keep from you, for it provides them with low interest money to use (misuse). But there are other reasons why over paying your withholding tax is a big mistake. If you were one of the people who received a refund, let's take a look at what could happen if you simply paid what was due and no more, and had those extra funds to invest each year.

If you invested $1,000 each year in a tax-sheltered plan for 30 years at 10% interest it would give you just under $165,000. That would be an exciting result from money that was yours all the time, but it also means that the $30,000 (30 years times $1,000) produced $135,000 of compound interest that the government was getting instead of you. Do you feel they deserve it? Then why let them use it?

What can you do about withholding tax? Take the necessary steps to review with your payroll department, the tax being deducted from your paycheque. When you started with your employer you were required to complete a TD1, which stated your marital status and the number of dependants you had. If you have been with this employer for a number of years, there is little doubt that some of these details have changed. Quite possibly you have married in the intervening time and now are struggling to support your ten kids. (Well at least one or two). Visit your payroll department and ask to review that form to be sure that ALL of the details on it are accurate. This simple review could provide extra dollars to your take home pay. If your RRSP, medical, or charitable contributions are substantial and consistent each year, you can contact your Revenue Canada office and get a waiver form which permits you to reduce your withholding tax based upon your record in these areas in the past years.

Whatever you do, do not delay, for this is money that is rightfully yours in the first place and we believe you will spend it more wisely than the government. Should you successfully arrange to have your withholding tax reduced, **please do not** go and simply spend those additional funds each month. Rather move them into a good tax-sheltered investment plan. You have managed to get along without that extra cash up until now, so you should be able to maintain the same lifestyle without additional hardship.

Remember, a refund is not a gift from Revenue Canada. It is money that is rightfully yours and should never have been in their hands to use in the first place.

"Compared to them I'm an amateur, and the thing about my jokes is that they don't hurt anybody. You can say they're not funny or they're terrible or they're good or whatever it is, but they don't do no harm. But with Congress—every time they make a joke it's a law. And every time they make a law it's a joke."

Will Rogers, author

SECRET 3

Paying "Only" Your Dues

As we said in Secret #2, do not permit Revenue Canada to use your money. Now we want to go one step further and suggest to you that you should not be giving them anymore than is due them. By this we mean you have a right (and we would say, obligation) to not pay any more tax than is absolutely due. Unfortunately, many people are paying more than they are actually required to pay because they do not have knowledge of some of the rulings in the tax code and as a result, do not take advantage of details that could reduce their taxes. Other chapters in the book will deal with plans and programs that the government has prepared for tax-deferral or tax-sheltered investing. In this chapter, we want to address small things that can have an effect on your tax return and if you are able to combine some of these, they can provide you with significant money for investing.

1. **Child Tax Benefit (CTB)** – Because the child tax benefit is essentially in the name of the child and is considered to be their income, if you deposit that monthly amount into an investment in their name, the earnings are reported in **their name**. This means that as long as the child's income is below the taxable income level these earnings are **TAX-FREE**. Although taking the CTB and investing it in an RESP (Registered Education Savings Plan) is one way of getting the money to grow **TAX-FREE**, we suggest that investing the money outside of the RESP is better. This is because withdrawing the funds from an RESP other than

for education, makes them subject to tax. Using this simple investing procedure permits you unrestricted access to the funds for whatever reason, and **TAX-FREE** until the investment earnings get to such a level that they are taxable. At that point an RESP or something similar can be started.

Let's look at some numbers. Investing the $100 each month for 18 years, even at only 5% interest, will provide about $35,000 that will have no restrictions on its use, and no tax problems from the earnings as long as the child's other combined earnings do not exceed the personal exemption ceiling. This will provide the same income as the RESP without the restrictions. However, you must be depositing **that child's** CTB cheques into **their account**.

2. **Pay your spouse's taxes** – Your continuing goal is always to, in as many ways as possible, bring the taxable income of the highest earning spouse down by moving income into the hands of the spouse with the lower tax rate. If additional investments by the higher income spouse are going to just increase the income of that spouse, why not take that money and pay the taxes for the lower-rate spouse and have the lower-rate spouse invest that same amount and let the earnings accrue. Your payment of this tax is not taxable to that spouse because it is viewed as a gift and could provide a nice nest egg.

3. **Deduct consultation fees** – If your tax return is prepared by someone who charges a fee, that amount can be a deduction. Also, any fees paid for investment or financial advice can be deducted from the income earned by these investments.

4. **Business Travel** – Should your employer require that you use your vehicle for some business travel, it is quite likely that they provide compensation for the distance traveled away from the office. However, the fact that you need to get your vehicle to work to make this trip can also be used as a deduction. Thus, travel to and from work that day, a trip that usually could not be deducted now becomes a valid expense. One word of caution. Be sure to document this very precisely and do not deduct an unreasonable amount. In an audit Revenue Canada will probably verify against your employer's records, that the dates match and the vehicle was actually used this way.

   If your employer needs you to pick-up something on your way to, or from work, such as the mail, this could also turn a regular trip into a deduction.

5. **Political Contributions** – We feel that one of the major quirks in our tax law is the political donation ruling. On the first $100 you donate to a political party the government gives you a credit of $75 on your tax return. So in actuality, the donation really only cost you $25. Again, we think this says more about the politicians than it does about the actual benefit of such a donation, but we guess this is probably the only way politicians can get anyone to donate to them.

6. **Deferred reporting** – If you have investments that mature on specific dates, work to schedule these in such a way that they mature early in January. That way, even though most of the income was earned in one year you do not have to take it into your income until the next and that gives you almost a whole year before having to deal with the tax on those earnings.

7. **Loans to Children** – As we've said, the goal is to move earnings from the tax return of the higher earner into the hands of someone with a lower or zero tax rate. You can do this with your children by giving them a loan. If the child is earning any wages at all, have **THEM invest that money** and declare the earnings on their tax return. Then as they need money for the things they want, you loan it to them interest free. We realize that this is not a good return for you, but your goal is to not have any more earnings added to your income. So instead of you investing, have the child invest their money and declare the earnings in their name, and pay little if any tax. With this simple strategy you have essentially moved earnings from a higher tax rate, to a lower one. **A word of caution**: You want to be sure that the relationship with your child is such that you are sure that the money will not be wasted in a way you do not want. Remember, this money is in their name and therefore legally out of your control, so why not have the investments require two signatures for access. This can easily be justified as long as the child is a minor, but double check with your financial planner for the best structure.

8. **Levies, fines and penalties** – "Which are incurred for the purpose of earning income are deductible business expenses." This was a Supreme Court decision in April, 1999. It came as a result of a taxpayer fighting the claim of Revenue Canada that they could not be deducted. Therefore keep the receipts and deduct the expense.

9. **Your business Acumen** – For years Revenue Canada disallowed many business and investment deductions because they said they did not pass the "reasonable expectation of profit" test. In other words, if you became

involved in a venture that did not produce the income you expected, you were not permitted to deduct the expense if Revenue Canada deemed that there was not a "reasonable expectation of profit". This made Revenue Canada the "judge" of whether or not such a venture could have produced a profit. May 23, 2002 the Supreme Court brought down a ruling that took this "right" away from Revenue Canada. They stated: "Where the nature of an activity is clearly commercial, there is not need to analyze the taxpayer's business decisions." The court further declared that this test "should not be used to second-guess the business judgment of the taxpayer. It is the commercial nature of the taxpayer's activity which must be evaluated not his or her business acumen". This means now the only test Revenue Canada can give to your deduction claim is whether it is related to personal use or activity, or a hobby. It was encouraging to have Revenue Canada removed as judge and jury on this, especially in light of how they build "washrooms".

10. **Cottage corporation** – Because your cottage is not your principal residence, if it is left in your estate at the time you die, even if you are passing it along to your children, it will need to be appraised and the capital gains on it added to your estate, along with all the tax ramifications. And then the fight will probably begin. Avoid all that. Set up a simple corporation now, while that asset can be valued at a reasonable figure and give the children shares in it. A good lawyer can do the job now for a reasonable fee and assist you in structuring it so that decisions can be made fairly and without a quarrel. If only all of life could be that simple!

Good Debt/
Bad Debt

A recent study of the figures from Stats Can showed that Canadians currently have one of the highest debt ratios ever. Combined household and mortgage debt is around 790 billion dollars, which means that for every $1 in disposable income we owe $1.16. In addition to that, the national savings rate is now 0%. This is not surprising, because we are needing to use all of our disposable income to pay for our debt. Part of this has resulted from the fact that over the past 10 years, food, real estate, insurance, cars, and energy have all increased significantly while the average family income has hovered around $60,000 with a very insignificant increase beyond that. This cannot go on indefinitely for eventually things will catch up to us just as they have in the housing meltdown in the US. Another result of this whole debt situation is that 50% of Canadians do not have any savings/investments for retirement and the other half have on the average $40,000, which in most cases does not even equal a year's salary. Corporate pensions are a thing of the past with only 30% of the population having them; so we are quickly becoming a nation that will be totally dependant on our government in our old age. As we have already discussed, the government is not taking good care of our money, so probably won't have much for us then. Something must be done by each and every one of us to address this problem, **now**! I cannot stress this enough.

In our opinion there are several steps that need to be taken:

1. Stop spending money. – This does not mean "not paying" your bills, but rather stop spending money on things that are not needed. Most likely many of these are being paid for with a credit card and probably on a card that gives some kind of points. We use the "points" to rationalize using the credit card instead of cash for the payment. Forget the points and if possible forget the purchase. Is this an item you really need, or simply want? Begin **paying for everything with cash**, and when you are out of the cash you have budgeted for, stop buying until the next paycheque.

2. Tabulate exactly how much you owe in debt other than your mortgage and start reducing that. – Make the minimum payment on those cards with the lowest interest rate and apply additional funds to the cards with the highest interest rate. You want to eliminate the debt on the highest interest credit cards first. This assumes that you have **stopped** using your credit cards entirely.

3. Once you have your cash flow and spending under control, you can now take the steps necessary to turn bad debt into good debt. What is the difference? Bad debt is any debt where you **cannot** use the interest charge as a deduction on your tax return.

There is only one kind of debt where you can use the interest charge as a deduction, and that is debt incurred to produce income whether passively through investments or actively through a business. In only these two cases can the interest costs of borrowing money be applied against the income being earned with that borrowed money. You simply pay tax on the difference.

How do you turn Bad Debt into Good Debt? Let's say you owe $5,000 on your credit card, but that you also have $8,000 that you have managed to set aside in an investment. If the investment is simply a certificate paying interest and you have just been compounding the interest, the procedure is quite simple. Redeem the portion of the investment needed and take that money and pay off your credit card debt. Then visit your bank and ask to borrow $5,000 to re-invest in the program you had been participating in. You may have to use some of the equity in your home as security, but that should be easy. The bank may also simply accept the certificate as security, but with the current turmoil in the markets they may want all $8,000 as their security for the $5,000 loan. No matter what – you have now changed bad debt into good debt because the interest on **this** debt can now be written off against the income that it is earning.

Some years ago a financial planner that I know called on a farmer in Saskatchewan, trying to interest him in a particular investment program. As they talked, the farmer said that he had all of his finances under control and that he did not need the help of a financial planner. In fact, he went on to say that in the slower winter months, he studied the Income tax act and bulletins, and as a result "took advantage of every tax break possible". Upon hearing this, my friend asked the farmer if he was deducting his house mortgage interest from his taxable income. The farmer retorted, "you can't do that!" My friend questioned further, stating that yes there is a way to do it and was he doing it? The farmer again claimed that he had studied every aspect to the income tax act and knew there was no way that Revenue Canada would permit that deduction. But then the farmer asked how it could be done. The response he received was, "If I can show you the way it can be done and you agree that it can work, will you listen to my investment proposal?" The farmer listened to the proposal and then invested in the program because he was so impressed with both pieces of information that were given to him. For much less than that investment, we are going to show you how it can be done. Mind you, that investment plan was a good one, but it is no longer available.

What did he tell this farmer, that the farmer could not learn from the Revenue Canada information? Probably something like the following illustration. This is very similar to turning bad debt into good debt.

"You quite likely have at least $100,000 invested in some plan somewhere. For easy figuring lets assume this and the following other factors; this money is invested at 4% and is producing interest income. Since interest earnings are taxable, and you appear to be a prosperous farmer, you will most likely be at a 40% tax rate. Therefore, the $4,000 interest will be taxed back in the amount of $1,600. This means that the net gain on that amount invested is actually only $2,400. If you are carrying a $100,000 mortgage on your home, we will assume that the interest rate on that mortgage is 6%. That means your mortgage is costing you $6,000 per year in interest. Let's work with these basic assumptions as we show how to make the $6,000 tax deductible. The first step is to cash in the $100,000 investment and use that money to pay off the mortgage. Now re-visit the bank and ask to borrow $100,000 using the mortgage free house as collateral. With the $100,000 loan you now receive, you repurchase the investments you turned into cash to pay off the mortgage. Because the income tax act permits you to deduct as an expense the **cost of money borrowed to earn income** from investing, this amount now becomes a tax deduction."

We realize this sounds very simple, and in actuality it really is!

Can anyone do this? Yes. However, not everyone is set up to act on this immediately. The main factor is your current debt situation. If your current debt situation is primarily your home mortgage and maybe a vehicle or two, and all of your credit cards are always paid in full each month, you are in a good position to change bad debt into good debt. If your investments are a LIRA, a RRSP, or a tax sheltered vehicle of some kind, the rollover will be more complicated because of the tax ramifications of removing any of those funds. In situations like that, it is vital that you work with your financial planner and follow his or her guidance. Because there are certain rules that must be observed in implementing such a plan and restrictions on how soon you can repurchase your original investments, it is crucial that you have your financial planner involved, and that you are confident that they know how to proceed within the rules on such a changeover.

Now let's look closer at the numbers. Before this maneuver, you paid the bank $6,000 in interest on your mortgage, and $1,600 to Revenue Canada in tax on your interest earning investment. With this plan in place you will be permitted to earn $6,000 in interest before you will have to start paying tax on it because, that is the cost of the money you borrowed to purchase the investments. Now instead of paying the bank $6,000 and Revenue Canada $1,600 tax, you pay the bank the $6,000 in interest. Because it reduces the tax you actually pay by that amount, you essentially have this money to invest and gain interest on. If you add this $7,600 to the investment each year, at the end of 10 years you would have about $95,000 in additional investments even at a low 4% rate.

So you can see what happens when you turn bad debt into good debt. Of course, if you place this money in an interest earning investment, you will have to pay tax on the interest you earn. If you are wise enough to take this course of action, you will undoubtedly be wise enough to place the funds into an investment that will be subject to a capital gains tax, which is much lower.

Now to leave you with a Smile. A Smile a Day calendar once had this quote. "**Only a banker and accountant wear a belt and suspenders both**." When you visit your accountant and/or loans offices at the bank, take note of this. It is interesting how true we have found this to be!

" **Borrow to Invest Save to Buy.**"

"The bad news is time flies. The good news is you're the pilot."

Michael Altshuler, speaker, author

"Life is not measured by the number of breaths we take, but by the moments that take our breath away."

Anonymous

RRSP
A Great Saving Tool

A few years ago a friend dropped into my business and since it was near the end of February, I asked him if he had all of his paperwork done for the last year's RRSP contributions. His reply was that he does not contribute to RRSPs or anything else for his retirement. My response was that all indications are that the way the government is mis-managing our pension plan, we could not count on anything from them. He did not disagree with me about the mis-management. With regards to counting on the government for pension, he said something to the effect that this was true, but our government will not leave anyone without, and those that have RRSPs will simply have their assistance from the government reduced accordingly. He made a point that I could not disagree with, however, I still could not agree with his course of action. Unfortunately, it seems that a lot of people agree with him, for statistics show that 93% of RRSP eligible contributions are **NEVER** made. We hope these people have another source of retirement investment in their portfolio.

All indications are that by the time most people who are reading this book reach retirement age, the Canada pension fund will be so under-funded, that the government will be looking at any other option, just to get a little money to offer to those on pension. What we mean by under-funded is that the current account balance and the projected earnings will not be enough to cover the total amount of pension that will have to be paid out to those who are entitled. At that point, there is only so much money that the government will be able to squeeze out of the earning public. For this reason we feel that although we have had to contribute to the Canada Pension Plan faithfully over the years, we are not going to see much, if any return of our investment. The government has used our contributions to subsidize the pensions of those who are drawing out a pension right now, for they are being paid far more than they ever contributed.

This makes the whole plan nothing more than a gigantic (**the biggest**) Ponzi scheme. With all of the current publicity and criminal charges against people who have promoted Ponzi schemes, the hypocrisy of a government that pursues those charges while actively perpetuating their own Ponzi program is farcical.

What is an RRSP? The tax department name is Registered Retirement Savings Plan and it is simply a program put in place by the government to encourage taxpayers to set aside money for their future retirement. However, keep in mind that it is only a **tax deferral** program. That means it permits you, within limits, to not pay the tax on the money now, with the hope that when you begin to withdraw the funds, you will be in a lower tax bracket and therefore end up paying less tax. Also, once the funds are placed into the plan, they can grow without any tax liabilities until you begin to withdraw them.

Let's look first at the advantages of making contributions. Again, the numbers we will be using are simply rounded off so that you can easily follow the logic of the plan. These numbers will vary considerably depending upon where you live and what your tax rate is, as well as many other factors. However, for this illustration we are going to use the numbers of $60,000 as your taxable income, and a tax rate of 40%. With these numbers we easily calculate that you are going to have to pay

$24,000 in income tax. However, if you decided to contribute $10,000 to an RRSP, your taxable income now drops to $50,000, and at 40% your tax is only $20,000. You now have $10,000 invested for you. If you do this every year and it grows at a rate of 10% per year, in 20 years you will have $630,000 available for your retirement. In addition, each year you have saved $4,000 in taxes, so in actuality your annual $10,000 really only cost you $6,000.

To see further advantages let's look at what happens if you do not shelter the investment from taxes. We will use the same numbers, but here is what happens. Because you first paid the tax on the $10,000, you really only have $6,000 to actually invest. Then because the income is not sheltered, you must pay additional tax on the earnings, which is deducted from the amount invested. The net result is that after 20 years you end up with about $240,000 instead of $630,000!

The RRSP has a great advantage, for even though you will have to pay the tax when you begin to withdraw from the plan, it permits you to reduce your tax now and allows the money to **compound tax – sheltered** over the years.

As we said at the beginning of this chapter, the under-funded pension liabilities that the government currently has, as well as those in most of our social programs, makes us very nervous about relying completely on Canada Pension Plan (CPP). One cannot rule out that at some point the government may change the rules on this program, but for now it is a great **tax deferral** tool.

RRSPs have been refined over the years to permit greater flexibility within them, and we are going to address a number of those refinements now. We caution you not to rush off and act on them without further study! We cannot address all of the nuances to each strategy, so suggest that you do them only in consultation with a competent financial planner.

1. **Self-Administered RRSP** – Although most people set up their RRSP through a financial planner, the act does permit you to administer the use of the funds yourself. However, we caution you about this. Be very sure that you understand the act thoroughly. A mis-step, could result in the withdrawal of the tax sheltered status, which would mean that you would have to pay the tax on all the earnings – the past as well as the current.

2. **Name your spouse as beneficiary** – This prevents a substantial loss of the funds to tax, should you die without taking care of this detail. If you fail to name a beneficiary, the whole amount in the RRSP becomes taxable in your estate at the time of your death. In such a case, it is quite possible that the government will get more of your RRSP than your heirs. The beneficiary can move the account over into their name without tax liabilities and merge the plans as they see fit. Note: You are limited to beneficiaries who are either your spouse or a dependant child.

3. **Contribute as early in the year as possible** – In the story at the beginning of the chapter, the conversation took place in late February. Most people do not think about any contributions for the previous tax year, until then. If you would make that contribution as early as possible in the tax year, you gain the interest of the whole year, and over 20 years at 10% that can amount to an extra $61,159. To make this less painful, why not have the contributions made automatically each month?

4. **Contribute for your spouse to their RRSP** – The tax act permits you to reduce your income by contributing a maximum amount to an RRSP, but it does not limit that

contribution to only your RRSP. It is possible to make that contribution to your spouse. The main advantage to this is that at the time you begin to make withdrawals, because you both have RRSPs, you can draw from each. Although your combined draw may total a reasonable amount, the taxable amount of each could be considerably lower than if only one recipient was taking the full amount. This is a way to split income in the future and save on the amount of tax that will have to be paid on that money.

5. **RRSP Home Buyers Option** – As mentioned, an RRSP is strictly a tax-deferral program, but it can also be used to assist you in making a first time home purchase. At present the act permits you to withdraw up to $25,000 from your RRSP to assist in the purchase of your first home. Your spouse can also do the same, so this could permit you to provide a down payment of $50,000. However there are two cautions here. You are required to repay the full amount in regular scheduled payments over the next 15 years, and secondly, keep in mind that this money is not earning while it is absent from the fund, so it could greatly reduce the final balance.

6. **Lifelong Learning Plan** – There is a Secret devoted to explaining RESPs but if you have not been participating in such a program, your RRSP can provide you with some funds to advance your education. As with the Home Buyers Option, to a maximum of $20,000, you can withdraw up to $10,000 per year for four years for you or your spouse's education at a qualifying institution. Also, like the Home Buyers Option, you are required to repay that money in regularly scheduled payments, beginning with the 5th year and to be completed 10 years after that. Once again we pass along the reminder that the absence of this money is going to affect the final balance.

7. **Advance contributions** – If you are having a lower income year than usual, but still have the funds to make a contribution, do it even if you do not claim the whole contribution. The balance of the amount not claimed can be carried forward, to be used in a year when your higher income gives you room to contribute. What we are saying, is get your money into that sheltered environment and working for you whenever possible.

8. **Retirement or Severance Packages** – If because of changes in the business climate you take an early retirement or a severance package or some other lump sum payments, talk to your financial planner to see how you can move these packages into the plan to increase the amount that is growing tax-sheltered.

We have provided several suggestions as to how to get the maximum amount of funds into your RRSP, and now we want to give you one final reminder as to how to keep the maximum amount of money growing for you – **Tax Sheltered**. Many funds have administrative fees that are charged for their work. These can vary from $0 to as high as $250. Pay these separately. Do not have them automatically deducted from the balance. Let me show you why. If the fees are $250 per year over 30 years at 10%, you would have about $45,000 more in your account by paying them separately rather than having them deducted. A little can make a big difference.

One other question that many financial planners are asked regarding an RRSP is; is it better to pay down my mortgage or contribute to my RRSP? The answer to that is primarily dependant upon the interest rate on your mortgage as related to the performance of your RRSP. Let's look at some numbers. If you have a $100,000 mortgage at 7.5% interest rate amortized over 25 years, your monthly payment on principal and interest will be about $739 per month. In order to pay off your mortgage in 15 years you would need to add $448 to your monthly payment for a total of $1,187 each month. However, by making this additional payment, you will save almost $55,000 in interest and if you can pay it off in 10 years, your interest saving will be just under $80,000.

Now let's go to the next step. If at the end of the 15 years you continued to make the payment (plus the savings gained from contributing to an RRSP) into your RRSP for another 15 years, you would end up with about $588,000 in your RRSP.

Which option is better? Paying off your mortgage is better if the rate of return on your RRSP is equal to, or lower than your mortgage interest rate. If your RRSP returns are substantially above your mortgage rate, continue to invest in RRSPs. Generally that rate needs to average at least 2% points higher than your mortgage interest rate for **ALL** the years of the investment, in order for it to be better than paying off your mortgage.

Just by the way, the same basic rule applies to any other debt that you may be servicing. A good rule of thumb is to get rid of the debt first, unless the investment guarantees a return above the interest rate you are paying on the debt.

This simple table summarizes the differences.

Years of Mortgage @ 7.5% interest	# Months Contributing to RRSPs	Amount Contributed Monthly	Tax Savings Monthly with RRSP	RRSP ending total after 25 years		
				5%	7.50%	10%
10	15 yrs x 12 = 180	$1,187	$356	$399,549	$483,608	$588,299
25	25 yrs x 12 = 300	$448	$134	$333,341	$474,779	$686,887

Expensive Investment Income

In our opinion, one of the most onerous taxes the government has created, is the situation where you pay the income tax on the money you earn, and by careful management and discipline you invest this money that you have already paid the tax on. Then, as those investments produce, **YOU HAVE TO PAY TAX ON WHAT THE INVESTMENTS EARN**. In our opinion this is excessive and blatantly unfair. That is part of the reason we try and provide you with information, which permits you to shelter as much of your investment income as possible. Not everything can be sheltered, however. Therefore, you want to be sure that your "non-sheltered investment earnings" are the type that give you a reasonable opportunity to increase without being subject to additional taxes. Investments generate income in basically 3 different ways with minor variations on each. They are: **capital gains**, **dividends**, or **interest**. Let's look at each of these items in more depth and then at a comparative chart showing the possible tax ramifications of each.

Interest – Through various loans that we have to repay, most of us are acquainted with the interest we pay for the use of that money. Earned interest is essentially the same thing; money paid to you for money that you have "loaned" to a bank in a savings account, or to some other organization or business, in forms such as promissory notes, GICs, bonds, treasury bills, or similar. Money earned in this way is considered to be the same as your earned income or wage and the tax is calculated as such on your tax return. This is almost always taxed at the highest rate possible.

We say almost always because Secret #9 is one slight exception to this rule.

Dividends – When corporations earn a profit, they are permitted to pay out a portion of that profit to people who own shares in the corporation. The money distributed from the profits are called dividends. Within a corporation there can be several classes of shares, but generally there are only two, **general** and **preferred**. The difference is simply that preferred shares receive special consideration should the corporation claim bankruptcy, and in the payment of dividends. Preferred shareholders have first claim on any assets in the event of a bankruptcy and they also often have an arrangement for a pre-determined dividend payment. In many ways the preferred share arrangement is similar to a debt interest payment or a bond. The crucial difference is in the way dividends are taxed. Because the corporation has already paid the tax on these profits before they are divided among the shareholders, you pay considerably less tax on this money when it comes into your hands.

Capital Gains – Many other investments do not have a set rate of return nor do they pay out profits or dividends. Usually they are structured in such a way that you invest some capital, either in an initial one time investment or through a series of contributions to the capital. These investments can be in anything from mutual funds to real estate. The main tax factor in these investments is that they do not make any dispersal (return money) into your hands while you own them. It isn't until you choose to sell them that you realize their value. At that time they become subject to Capital Gains tax, which is simply a tax on the gain of the capital invested.

Here is a very simple illustration of how it works. Let's say that you invested $10,000 capital into a piece of real estate and within a short period of time that piece of property was sold for $50,000. The capital gains is the difference between the adjusted cost base (ACB) of $10,000 and the $50,000. The resulting $40,000 (less any expenses incurred) is the capital gain and according to the tax act you are only taxed on 50% of the amount, but at your current tax rate. So in other words, you would only have to pay tax on $20,000.

You will note that timing could be an important factor in the completion of such a transaction, for if this capital gain could be taken into your hands at a point when your income is relatively low, it could be subject to a lower tax rate. However, with many of these investments you may not be able to co-ordinate it so that you can exit at both a time of lower income and a high market value for the investment.

Your personal residence is one exception to this capital gains ruling. The tax code permits you to receive **TAX-FREE** any gains that you may make on the sale of your principal residence. You are only permitted to receive this tax break once a year, but if you have the ability to spot a real estate bargain and can improve the property while living in it for at least a year, this could be a way to significantly increase your capital, **TAX-FREE** over a number of transactions.

So we can see that tax wise, interest income is generally not the best way to invest your money, and if you can move interest investments to ones that pay dividends instead, it can significantly lower your tax bill and therefore your net return. Preferred shares or investments that hold preferred shares, are the "preferred" way to go if you are looking for something more secure. If you are a very cautious investor and feel more comfortable with Guaranteed Income Certificates (GICs), or bank interest, you may want to consider purchasing actual bank shares. These are very secure and we continually hear about the incredible profits banks make, so why not get a piece of that action instead of the little interest they are willing to pay you for using your money and take advantage of dividend investment income instead of interest.

In closing this chapter we want to illustrate more clearly the advantages of moving from interest earnings to dividends. Let's say that right now you are in the highest tax rate bracket. Depending on the province in which you live, this will vary, but for ease of calculation we will use a 45% tax bracket. If you receive interest income of $10,000 you will have to pay the government $4,500 of that in tax. If that $10,000 was received as dividend income the tax rate would be only 25% or $2,500. This provides you with an extra $2,000 to spend or re-invest, since you do not have to give it to the government. If you re-invested that $2,000 each year at 10% in a tax-sheltered program, at the end of 20 years you would be ahead by about $126,000.

As you are aware, throughout this book we are constantly looking for ways to get funds into your hands **TAX-FREE**. Changing from interest income to dividend income with the help of your financial planner is a great way to reduce your taxes, but additional planning can get most, if not all, of these dividends into your hands **TAX-FREE**. How? Every province has set a personal and dividend tax credit that permits you to take a set amount of dividend income into your hands **TAX-FREE**. Learn what the rate is for your province and then get in touch with your financial planner and begin to save even more tax.

Interest income?

Dividend income?

Capital gains?

You know what your risk tolerance is and now you know better, which method could work best for you and which you would be the most comfortable with.

> **"If there is no wind, row."**
>
> Latin Proverb

> **"The greatest obstacle to discovering the shape of the earth, the continents, and the oceans was not ignorance but the illusion of knowledge."**
>
> Daniel J. Boorstin, historian, professor, attorney, and writer

SECRET 7 The BEST Tax Shelter

Most of us view insurance as a "necessary evil". What if we could show you that not only is insurance a good thing to have in case of your death, but that it could also provide you with a way to grow and use money **Tax-Free**. In the chapter on RRSPs we talked about how you can shelter your money and let it grow within the RRSP, without any tax liabilities until you begin to take the money out. Hopefully, by that time you will be in a lower tax bracket and therefore get to pay the tax at a lower rate. However, **Life Insurance Tax Shelters** (LITS) offer another option that will not only permit your money to grow **Tax-Free**, but if structured properly, will permit you to access the funds without tax ramifications. So instead of just a Tax Deferral you can have **Tax-Free** money. Are you interested? Without a doubt!

First let's understand what **LITS** are. Each insurance company has their own name for their unique plan, but the plans basically operate like this. You participate in an insurance plan that also permits you to deposit money into it. The amount deposited can be very flexible and may change as you desire over the years, however, you will always be required to participate in the insurance coverage. Our recommendation is that you subscribe to the lowest "decreasing term" possible. You want your actual insurance premiums to be the lowest necessary to keep the plan active, because you want to take the extra money and deposit it within the plan as an investment.

Revenue Canada gives these plans a tax "exempt" status as long as they meet the criteria described in the tax act. The amount of life insurance required is based upon a Revenue Canada formula and each year every plan must pass that test, so you can be assured that the program meets the Revenue Canada requirements.

Why are these plans better than other non-sheltered investments? Because:

1. They permit your money invested in the plan to grow **TAX-FREE**.

2. The annual maintenance fee for the plan is considerably less than the tax that would have to be paid on earnings on the investments that were not sheltered.

This illustration may help. Although the numbers will not be the same for you, it should give you a good idea of the benefits of such a plan. Suppose your investments are earning a rate of 10% annually and each year you deposit $10,000 into a non-sheltered investment of some kind with your tax rate at 40%. At the end of 20 years you would have $630,025 in the plan, but if you had to pay the tax on these investment earnings each year, you would have also paid a total of about $172,010 in tax. If you are able to shelter that money in an LITS, those earnings will be the same but because the funds are growing within the plan there are no tax liabilities. Over the 20 years the administrative fees for the plan will probably be somewhere slightly over $20,000, so by participating in the plan you saved an additional $150,000 in tax that you did not have to pay.

Probably you are saying, "that is all well and good, but when I want to take the money out we have the same problem as with the RRSP". Not quite. If you choose to begin to withdraw the funds directly into your hands, you will be permitted to take out the adjusted cost base (ACB) of the plan minus the cost of the insurance, without any tax problems. So in other words you will be able to take out just under $200,000 ($10,000 times 20 years less the insurance premiums) **TAX-FREE**.

With the balance of the money you have two withdrawal options. The first option is straight forward and structured in the same way as withdrawals from RRSPs. Selecting that option means there will also be taxes to pay.

The second option is what makes LITS **the GREATEST Tax Shelter** available in Canada. Instead of withdrawing the money, visit your bank (your insurance company may also do this for you) and borrow money using the policy as the security. Generally, do not borrow the full amount **all** at one time, but annually as you have need of it. The arrangement you make for the loan is that no repayment will ever be made on it, but at the time of your death the funds from the LITS will be used to cover the total owing. This permits you to access the earnings from this money Tax-Free because loans have no tax ramifications and so the money is totally yours.

TAX-FREE

Upon your death, because the plan is an insurance policy, your loan is paid in full, and the remainder plus the insurance, flows to your beneficiary without any tax assessment at all. Again **TAX-FREE!** Things don't get much better than that.

The lending company will feel comfortable with this arrangement because they know that their loan is well secured (by the balance you have in the fund plus the insurance) and that funds are continuing to grow. So everyone is happy.

Again let's look at some possible numbers with these two options.

If you select the first option – you will have accumulated somewhere around $630,000 in the plan. Your total direct contribution was $200,000. However, you had to pay for the insurance coverage, so let's say that amounts to $60,000 over the 20 years. This means that you can immediately draw out $140,000 without any taxes being due. That would be the ACB. After that $140,000 has been withdrawn any additional funds would be subject to tax based upon your tax rate of the year in which you make the withdrawal.

If you choose the second option – and borrow against the funds rather than withdraw them, here is what could happen. You could take your first loan of $50,000 and then each year you increase it by 3% to account for inflation. Even doing that it will take you 24 years to borrow the total amount accumulated.

This simple chart shows the difference.

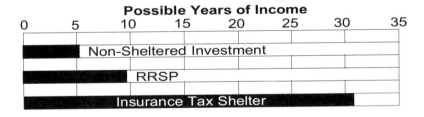

Remember that this money is flowing into your hands **Tax-Free** and in addition, in the event that you do not survive as long as the money does, because it is an insurance policy the balance remaining plus the insurance benefit moves into the hands of your beneficiaries **TAX-FREE**. Now you see why we say it is

The BEST TAX SHELTER!

" **Discovery consists of looking at the same thing as everyone else and thinking something different."**

- Albert Szent

8 Business Expenses Can Save You Taxes

> **" Work for profits, not wages."**
>
> - Jim Rohn

When Jim Rohn was 25 years of age, someone made the above simple statement to him and became his mentor. By the age of 31, Jim Rohn was a millionaire and since has gone far beyond his first million. No one has to tell you that the economy of the world is changing in very dramatic ways. The rapid increase in the cost of oil products alone is affecting, and will continue to affect, every aspect of our lives from where we work, to the holidays we can afford to take. One of the results of this change is the move from large, top-heavy corporations to small independent businesses. In 1994, only 57% of the people employed were considered to be working for a large business (over 300 employees) and that number is rapidly decreasing as the economy changes. What are your options?

Even though change is often frightening we believe that the move to small independent business is a great way to give a person flexibility in their work and also in their finances. A sole proprietorship, or home based business, can provide you with many tax breaks that you could never use while working for a large corporation. This change in the economy is giving the entrepreneurially-minded person the opportunity to begin to work for themselves by contracting out the knowledge and experience they have. Maybe this option, is available to you and with it the opportunity to become self-employed.

Why do we recommend this? Because it presents the opportunity of turning a portion of general-living expenses into a business expense, which can then be deducted from income. If your business is operated from a room in your home, that percentage of your home costs can be recorded as a business expense. Need to run out to the store for something? If there is an item you need to purchase for your business as well, the trip can then be recorded as a business trip. Or better yet, when you have a business trip to make, stop and take care of the personal things you might need. Also, when it comes to compensation from the business, you can structure it in such a way as to best suit your needs and use of the tax laws. There are many more things that could be added to this list of examples but we believe you get the idea. As always, it is important that you keep detailed records, in case of an audit by Revenue Canada. A careful recording of the date and time of the trip and the nature of the business taken care of on the trip should be proof enough that it was an actual business expense.

Don't have a business yet? Again, there are an infinite number of options out there, from home-based businesses, to consultants who travel to work under contract in an established business. There are people who make their living simply via the internet, either buying & selling on the internet, or serving as a go between for people who are searching for a particular product or information. To a great extent you are only limited by your imagination. We know of people who have turned their hobby into a small business on the side, and that business eventually grew to become their main source of income, which allowed them to leave their established workday world.

If you do not consider yourself a self-starter and need the structure of an 8 to 5 workday environment, this may not be for you. However, a person that turned their hobby into a business found that because of their love for the product and what they were doing, it was easy to go to "work" and they put in a lot more time than the 40 hour work week they previously did. They "worked" harder doing something they loved, so hardly considered it work.

> " You can have anything you want as long as you help enough people get what they want.."
>
> - Zig Ziglar

This is a good point from which to start a business. What do you know, or know how to get, that other people may want? It may simply be information or knowledge on some particular subject that could make you an "expert". It may be the ability to build or construct a product at a better price than some one else. It may be an experience which has provided you with knowledge that others are willing to pay for. For example, we know of a couple who sub-contracted to have their dream home built. From this experience, they learned what to do and what not to do, in working with sub-contractors. In addition they were able to compile a book describing their experience and how others could learn from it. This leads me to an area where we could provide experience other than the information in this book. Twice now, we have self-published a book, so from those experiences, we could almost write another book telling how it can be done and what things to avoid. Information and/or knowledge is wanted and needed in so many areas, both in a simplified form and also as a consultant.

The following websites and magazines could be a good starting point but a simple "Google" search will give you thousands of sites to explore for ideas. Google is another fantastic example of a couple of college students who found a need, took the knowledge they had and turned it into a business.

1. **www.startupinternetmarketing.com** Internet commerce is growing at a rate of 17% a year and is the ideal home business for in most cases it can be started with the tools you currently are using for fun. Your computer.

2. **www.bcentral.ca** Microsoft started in a university dorm room and today …! It is interesting that they have a website that provides ideas and tools for a person to start a small business.

3. **www.entrepreneur.com** *Entrepreneur* magazine has been around for a number of years and provides excellent information and links to other websites that are designed to help the self-employed or small business owner.

4. **www.inc.com** As a subscriber to *Inc.* magazine we found the information they provided invaluable. It is so helpful in giving you ideas on how to improve your business and how to look at things from a different perspective to enhance the quality of service you are providing.

5. **www.bas.cbsc.org** Before you actually start your business this is a good site to visit for the topics they cover show you how to investigate your potential market, a source for financing if needed, write a business plan, and how to structure your business.

We will now give a simple overview of some options to consider when setting up your business.

In the June/July 2008 issue of *Success* magazine, there are several different articles about business, with suggestions of how to get started, what type of business might interest you, and where to look to get started. To even share an abbreviated version of the many ideas included in the article would take up too much of this book. Therefore, we suggest that you visit **www.success.com** and track down that issue. We would like to go one step further and recommend that you subscribe to the magazine as soon as possible. We do not know of a better magazine for ideas and inspiration to help you attain the goals you have written down.

When first venturing into business, you need to look at which business structure would best suit you. There are three basic business structures, and of course, each has advantages and disadvantages in how they can be used and how they are taxed. Of course the tax area is the one we are most interested in for this book and so will primarily address those.

Sole Proprietorship – This is the simplest structure. In a sole proprietorship, the business is only you, and all expenses and income are factored into your income tax in the year they are generated. You are responsible for all the debts and obligations of the business, which could also mean that in the event things did not go well with your venture, any creditors or law suits could lay claim to any and all assets that you may personally possess;

including your house. This is a good business structure to use when first testing the waters, but we suggest that as the business grows, you at some point roll the business over into a corporation (for reasons we will share later). However, do not forget to roll it over into a corporation if the business really grows, because moving assets down the road can have some tax liabilities for your personal tax if they have increased in value.

Partnership – This is just what it says. It is sort of like combining two or more Sole Proprietorships into one. All of the obligations, debt, and income are shared in the same ratio as the partnership agreement sets out, but all partners are personally liable. In the case of a failure the ratio presented in the partnership agreement will not matter if someone has fewer assets than their share of the liability. The creditor can simply demand full settlement from any or all of the partners.

As you will have noted, we have mentioned a "partnership agreement" a couple of times. In a partnership the most important factor is that an agreement **MUST** spell out **ALL** of the contributions from each partner, both financial and sweat equity (how much work they put into the business), and how obligations and income will be shared. In addition, there should be a formula which explains how a partner can leave the partnership, and what claim he might have to the value of the business. We cannot over emphasize how vital such a document is and how crucial it is to have a lawyer who knows what they are doing, prepare it. Many a marriage and/or good friendships have been destroyed because they went into business together. Partnerships can be difficult but there can also be advantages because the various partners often bring to the business their own special expertise.

Tax wise a partnership has all of the same rules as a sole proprietorship, except that the deductions and income are shared (applied) proportionately by each of the partners.

Corporations – These structures are a little more complicated to setup and maintain because they are in actuality separate "entities" from any of the people involved. The owners in a corporation are known as shareholders, and that is exactly what they are. They hold a "share" of the corporation, but the corporation alone is responsible for the liabilities and obligations. As a separate entity the corporation is responsible for filing its own tax return and as a small business could take advantage of the special tax breaks offered to small businesses. On an income of up to $400,000 the tax could be as low as 16% depending upon which province the business is located in. The corporation meets that obligation out of its profits and then the shareholders are paid a dividend, which flows into their hands differently than other income, because it is from a Canadian corporation. In fact the shareholders could receive as much as $37,500 **Tax-Free** and additional dividend payments at a preferential tax rate.

Often tax advisors and accountants suggest that you not receive all of your income as dividends because it reduces the ceiling that you have for RRSP and Canada Pension Plan contributions, which down the road will affect your benefits in those areas. However, give their advice on this careful study, for tax savings now could give you other more flexible options for sheltering income such as a **Life Insurance Tax Shelter** (LITS). When you make this decision, have your accountant show you **ALL** of the options, so you can make an informed decision. If nothing else, get your accountant to read this book and especially become knowledgeable on LITS.

Many small business owners often become so involved in the day-to-day details of running their business that they fail to take time to adequately keep aware of tax changes or plan for the long term. Many feel that their accountant will keep them advised, but in most cases the accountant only "reports" what has taken place in the business. Seldom do accountants give advice on how to structure items to receive a maximum tax advantage or what changes could or should be made to maximize deductions and reduce your tax. This is why it is crucial that you find some source for this information, or ask your accountant a lot of questions. If your accountant is a small business owner himself, you have an advantage, for he will be able to provide some of the answers from his personal experience.

If your business is successful, and we hope it is, and grows far beyond your first expectations, there is one final **Tax-Free** claim you can make. When selling the business you can claim up to $750,000 as capital gains exemption, which moves that amount into your personal hands without tax ramifications. If you are doubly fortunate in that your marriage survived the venture and your wife was a partner in it, you can double that $750,000 to $1.5 million. Now you have different tax problems as you seek a way to invest this money, but what nice problems to have.

> "The secret of business is to know something that nobody else knows."
>
> Aristotle Onassis

> "Success in business requires training and discipline and hard work. But if you're not frightened by these things, the opportunities are just as great today as they ever were."
>
> David Rockefeller (1915

Tax-Free Savings Account

We now want to introduce a new set of 4 letters into your tax vocabulary. The budget of 2008 made an interesting addition to the **Tax-Free** earning options beginning in 2009. Whether this is directly a result of the Stats Can statistics indicating that Canadians currently have a $0 saving rate, or for some other reason we are not sure. Maybe the government is just getting concerned that the pool of funds within Canada that they need to access for their excessive borrowing, is getting too small. Anyway they have offered a plan that appears to be well worth participating in. The **Tax Free Savings Account** (TFSA are the 4 letters) permits you to set aside money and have it grow **Tax-Free**; and then permits you to access the funds without having to pay tax on the withdrawals. In our opinion this is one of the best programs that has come out of the government in a long time.

Here is how we understand it works. If you are 18 years of age or older you are permitted to set up a TFSA in much the same way you establish your RRSP. It has to be duly registered with the government as a TFSA. Each year you will be permitted to contribute up to $5000, (increasing each year adjusted for inflation) to the account, to grow **Tax-Free**.

There are three very attractive aspects to this program.

1. Even though you have to pay the tax before placing the money within the plan, there is no tax liability when withdrawing the funds, however, you cannot deduct the contributions from your income as you do with your RRSP.

2. You can have more than one plan but are limited to the $5,000 annual contribution ceiling.

3. After registering the account, if for some reason you are not be able to contribute the full $5,000 in a particular year, you can carry the unused balance forward and use it in the next years. If you select to withdraw a portion of that money during the year you can do that without tax problems and then return it at any point without affecting the contribution limit. In other words if you decided that you needed to use $1,000 for any purpose you can withdraw it and your contribution limit for that year is now $6,000.

This illustration may help. If you open the plan and in the first year are able to contribute the full $5,000 you will have used up your maximum contribution amount. However, if in year 2 you only contribute $3,000 this means that in year 3 you now have an amount of $7,000 that you can contribute. If in year 3, you were not able to contribute anything, but also withdrew $2,000, this would mean that in year 4 you could make up the difference which would now be $14,000 (That amount comes from 4 years times $5,000 minus the $5,000 and $3,000 contributed in years 1 & 2, plus the $2,000 withdrawn in year 3.)

Should you receive an unexpected inheritance or some other lump sum payment, this is an excellent way to invest it and still have the flexibility of being able to access it if needed. As stated, any amounts withdrawn **are not** included in income and therefore are not "taken into account in determining eligibility for income-tested benefits or credits delivered through the income tax system (for example, the Canada Child Tax Benefit, the Goods and Services Tax Credit and the Age Credit). Nor will such amounts be taken into account in determining other benefits that are based on the individual's income level, such as Old Age Security benefits, the Guaranteed Income Supplement or Employment Insurance benefits".

As with your RRSP there are certain restrictions as to where the investments can be made, but basically the same rules for RRSPs apply for TFSAs. Here are a few of the things you can or cannot do with this type of account.

- You can use the account as security for a loan from an established institution.

- You can give the funds to your spouse to invest and the earnings will accrue to him or her and not to you.

- In the event of your passing, all earnings in the plan previous to that date will not be subject to tax, but earnings after that date will be.

- In the event of a dispute, Revenue Canada will determine exactly how much contribution room there is based upon your previous year's tax returns.

- Should there be a divorce and in the settlement it is decided that some of the funds in a TFSA should be paid to the other spouse, these amounts can be moved into another TFSA without any tax liability.

As stated the nicest aspect of the plan is that the funds grow **TAX-FREE** and have no tax liabilities when withdrawn.

TAX-FREE growth and
TAX-FREE withdrawals!

A fantastic idea! We just hope that in the future, should there be a change of government, that they not change the program too much. Probably we are sounding a little paranoid, but we were assured that Income Trusts would NOT be taxed by the new government. So who can trust the promise of a politician?

A Tax-Free Savings Account!

> " If you would be wealthy, think of saving as well as getting."
>
> - Benjamin Franklin

> " The avoidance of taxes is the only intellectual pursuit that carries any reward."
>
> - Maynard Keynes

10 Begin Saving NOW For Your Child's Education

Statistics indicate that individuals who complete their post secondary training, will on the average in their life time earn a million dollars more than their non-educated companion. We all want this quality of life for our children but as one looks at sending them to university or college, we become concerned about what sacrifice we are going to have to make so that our children can get this education. Thankfully the government is willing to give us some tax breaks to assist us in accumulating the funds that will be needed, in a **Registered Education Savings Plan** (RESP).

Here is how it works.

Anyone, parent, grandparent, relative or friend can open the plan in the name of the child. The funds in the plan grow **Tax-Free** until they are used. Of course the more you set aside and the earlier you start, the higher the amount that accumulates. (Remember the illustration in Secret 3.) If you have saved the full child tax benefit (again we suggest that you review Secret 3) from the time the child was born, even using a very conservative rate of 5% you would have approximately $35,000 in the account by the time that child completes high school at the age of 18. A balance like that, will assist you in putting your child through a number of years of university without putting stress on the family finances at the time.

Further, if you are saving for your child's education, the Government of Canada will help you with special saving incentives that are only available if you have an RESP, including the **Canada Education Savings Grant** and the **Canada Learning Bond**. If you live in Alberta you may also be able to get an additional grant under the **Alberta Centennial Education Savings Plan**.

Your financial planner or any institution that is currently handling your investments, can set up such a plan and give you direction as to which plan is best for your situation. i.e., family plans, individual plans, or group plans. More on that once we have explained the basics of the plans.

The various plans:

1. **Family Plan**

   The family plan requires that the children be related to you either as children, grand children or adopted children. This option permits you to place all or any of the children into one plan to become the beneficiary down the road. That way if one or more of the children decides that further education is not for them, those funds can be redirected and used by any of the other children that do pursue more education. The government also permits that such a plan can be self administered, if you feel comfortable with handling the investing yourself. Regular scheduled contributions are not required. In many ways this plan permits some of the greatest flexibility.

2. **Individual Plan**

   This plan permits a person to set up a plan for one individual who is not related to you. Most of the other terms apply, but the key here is that the plan can only be for that one person who is not related to you. Should they choose not to go on to further their education, special arrangements will have to be made to collapse the fund, and there will be tax ramifications in doing that.

3. **Group Plan**

   These are set up by RESP dealers, who pool the funds from children of the same age and invest and administer them for the group. The arrangements vary of course, but this permits the beneficiaries to access their share of the benefits and the advantages of a larger pool of funds invested. Unfortunately the payout available depends upon how many beneficiaries are drawing out at the time. Only one child can be enrolled in each plan and they may or may not be related to you. Most of these plans require a regular scheduled contribution, usually monthly. Should the child decide not to use the funds there are withdrawal terms for the contributor and these of course will have tax ramifications.

Accessing the Funds

Once the beneficiary is enrolled in a qualifying institution or program, he or she can have access to the funds in the RESP under certain conditions.

They are as follows:

➢ The program is one recognized by the government as a legitimate education program.

➢ The program is at the least 3 weeks long and has a minimum of 10 hours of instruction each week.

➢ The program can include apprenticeships, and programs offered by a trade school, college or university.

If you have any concerns or questions about the qualification of the education program the child is considering, contact the RESP department at Revenue Canada to be sure it is approved. However be sure to get a written verification from that department before enrolling, so that you can prove that the plan does meet the demands of the government. (From our experience, do not rely on a simple verbal response on the telephone. This does not hold up in a dispute with Revenue Canada.) If the program selected fails to meet the government requirements, the funds withdrawn become taxable in your or the child's hands.

Since each plan has different regulations regarding withdrawals, be sure to get direction from your financial planner as to how you can withdraw the funds within the plan's terms when the child is ready to move on to additional education.

All plans are limited to 35 years, which means that if the funds have not been used up by that time, they must be moved into the hands of the beneficiary or contributor and are subject to all applicable taxes at that time. However, should this become necessary the tax code does provide the option of moving the funds directly into an RRSP without tax liability, where they can continue to grow tax-sheltered. If the government has provided grants at any point in the plan, their portion will be factored out and returned to them.

> " If you think education is expensive,
> try ignorance."
>
> — Derek Bok

> " If you would thoroughly know anything,
> teach it to others."
>
> — Tryon Edwards

11 Getting Maximum Help For Your Disability

Although most of us are not dealing with the situation of living with a child or family member who is disabled, Stats Can reports that over 12 percent of the families in Canada do have a family member who has an "activity limiting disability". In 2001, this was 3.6 million Canadians. In many cases they are totally dependant upon their supporting families for assistance in their living. In the back of the mind of these supporting individuals, no doubt is the question "what will happen if I am no longer here or cannot provide the support my loved one's needs in the future?".

Fortunately, the government realized that such a situation might evolve and provided for a way to help these care givers reduce their concerns about the future. As stated in the legislation, the purpose of "the **Registered Disablity Savings Plan** (RDSP) is to provide for the long-term financial security of a beneficiary who has a prolonged and severe physical or mental impairment". Again, as in many plans of this nature, the purpose of this program is to permit the funds to grow **tax-sheltered** within the plan. Parents, family members or other authorized contributors may contribute to the plan but their contributions are not tax deductible. As the beneficiary withdraws the funds, they become taxable in their hand at their tax rate, however the original contributions will not be taxable (ACB), only the earnings on the contributions. What this means is that if the fund has

$200,000 in it but $75,000 of that money is the contribution made by various individuals, no tax will need to be paid on the withdrawal of that $75,000. Only after that amount has been taken out will there be tax payable on the withdrawals. With careful planning a person can declare the withdrawals to be partially earnings and partially contributions so that the best tax advantage can be used for a number of years.

To assist in the plan, the government will also supplement the contributions from the Canada Disability Savings Grant program, based upon the income level of the contributors. These grants will match RDSP contributions with rates of 100%, 200%, or even 300% depending on the contributors income level up to a total of $70,000. For families with income under $74,357 the grant will match 300% of the first $500 and 200% on the next $1,000. So in other words, if your family can contribute $1,500 to the RDSP the government will add $3,500. This $5,000 can then grow **Tax-Sheltered** for many years. If your income is over the $74,357 the government will only match the first $1,000 but this in itself can be a great help. Please note that these amounts are in 2007 dollars and allowance has been made to raise the thresholds based upon inflation.

We will not go into the details as to what conditions need to be met for a person to qualify as a beneficiary because that would take too much space. The Income Tax Act section 118.3 gives a comprehensive explanation. Therefore, we would suggest that you study this section carefully if you believe that your family member might be able to take advantage of this program on an even limited basis, or if their doctor has indicated that the problem they are now dealing with might be long term. It is our experience that many people think they do not qualify for this program, when in actuality they do. **Do not miss out on this assistance from the government!**

The plan, as currently stated, does limit the total amount that can be contributed to $200,000 and no contribution can be made after the beneficiary reaches the age of 59. However, with these contributions growing tax sheltered and with supplementing grants from the government, the plan could accumulate a reasonable balance to ease the minds of the care givers in regards to the future. In addition the amounts paid out of a RDSP will not be factored into declared income for tax purposes and thus will not be taken into account for the purpose of calculating income-tested benefits, such as Child Tax Benefit, GST credits, Old Age Security or Employment Insurance benefits.

Lowest income families (if your 2007 income was less than $20,883) can get further assistance from Canada Disability Savings Bonds. These bonds provide up to $1,000 per year into a RDSP up to a maximum of $20,000 and are not dependant upon any contributions to the RDSP. The only influencing factor here is the income level of the family. There are two income levels that cannot be exceeded for the qualifying bond and the bonds will not be available once the beneficiary reaches the age of 49. If the family income is between $20,883 and $37,178, there is a graduated payment of these bonds, but there are funds available, so look into it if you feel your income level permits you to qualify.

One inconvenience that you should be aware of and keep in mind, is that all bonds, grants and the resulting investment income from these two items of assistance must be repaid to the government if any one of the following three events occur within 10 years after receiving them. They are:

➣ the death of the beneficiary

➣ the cessation of the beneficiary's eligibility

➣ the payment of income to the beneficiary from the plan.

Why the government has included this "claw back" clause into the plan is beyond us, but it is there and we want you to be aware of it. However, do not let it frighten you away from taking advantage of some great assistance in a difficult situation.

Using all of the programs and assistance available, a family with an income of less than $20,833 could receive as much as $4,500 per year from the government while needing to contribute only $1,500. If the family income crosses that threshold the amount available is only $500 less until $37,178, and again $500 less until $74,357. After that income level there is quite a reduction in assistance. However, just because there is not help from government grants, does not mean that a person should not have a plan after that income level. The amount set aside still grows **tax sheltered** until withdrawn.

In addition to these programs from the federal government, many of the provinces and territories also provide income support for people with disabilities. Although these are subject to a "means test" an RDSP in most cases does not affect that support.

As you consult with your financial planner about which RDSP will work best for you, be sure to ask him what he knows about both federal and provincial government programs that provide capital assistance for renovations for physical accessability for people with disabilities. If he can give you direction on this as well, then you know that he is knowledgeable about the program he is proposing for you.

We believe there a lot of people who have minor disabilities who think this secret **does not** apply to them, however the definition of "disability" in the tax act is very comprehensive. If you have any sort of disability, we suggest that you visit the CRA website at **www.cra-arc.gc.ca/tx/ndvdls/sgmnts/dsblts/menu-eng.html** and answer the questions that pop up when you click on "Are you eligible for the disability "amount"? After reviewing the information at this site, talk to your financial planner as to how it applies to you. Begin today to set your mind at ease for the future.

> **" The big secret in life is that there is no big secret. Whatever your goal, you can get there if you're willing to work."**
>
> - Oprah Winfrey

I.O.U. – Family Loans
(Happy Spouse – Unhappy Taxman)

As explained and illustrated earlier in this book, families where the income is split usually have a great tax advantage over a situation where only one partner is bringing home most of the income. Even though the total income may be the same in each case, the splitting of the income can substantially reduce the tax paid. At the risk of being tedious, your goal is to reduce the taxes you pay by as much as possible through legal and legitimate methods and income splitting is one of the most effective ways. However, the Taxman generally hates income splitting for it reduces the amount of tax they can collect from you. So if you earn the majority of the income in the household and your spouse substantially less you may think "I will simply give some money to my partner to invest and then let their investments earn income that would then be taxable to them" (lower income, lower tax rate). Careful now! As already stated the Taxman wants to collect as much tax from you as possible and they set the rules. An informal loan or giving of the money to a spouse for them to invest may trigger the tax codes "Attribution Rule". This rule simply summarized, states that if such a transaction is not done at 'arms-length' the Taxman will attribute the earnings back to the party that provided the funds. If this course of action is not implemented correctly, the taxes of the partner that loaned the money just got higher in spite of their effort to split the income.

The Taxman won again!
Don't give up there is a way to do it.

Before we look at the rules for structuring, let's take a look at the advantages of such an arrangement. We will use numbers once again, but always keep in mind that these are only examples and will change and vary depending on your tax situation, the province you are in, and the whims of the government.

For ease of understanding, say one partner alone earns $70,000 per year. The tax they would have to pay on that amount would be somewhere around $12,000. Now we will change the scenario a little. Let's keep the household income at $70,000 but have your spouse and yourself each earn $35,000. Your combined tax bills would be closer to $10,000. That is why, as stated early in this book, your goal is to always seek to reduce your income to the very lowest amount to keep you from moving up to a higher tax bracket. Remember your primary goal is to keep your tax bracket and the tax you pay, as low as possible.

It would be nice if the spouse who earns the highest income could simply say "I want to share this with my partner" and split the income as explained in the second scenario and save the household the $2.000 in tax. However, the CRA rules of attribution do not permit that, and the tax is always assessed against the person who actually earned the income or received the pay cheque. But do not despair, although you may not be able to split this earned income there are ways to effectively split investment income.

Let's construct a possible scenario using the numbers above.

To help keep things straight we will call the couple Ron and Carol. Ron earned $70,000 last year and paid tax of $12,000 on that amount. Carol earned no income and therefore paid $0.00 in tax. If Ron had a $100,000 investment earning 10% interest (I know these are hypothetical numbers but bear with me.) that $100,000 would earn $10,000 in interest. But that $10,000 of interest income would then be added to Ron's income, resulting in an added tax bill of about $4,000. Over a number of years the interest earnings could be substantial but the problem with this arrangement is that the government would be taxing a lot of it away. Ron wants to split income with Carol. With Carol having no other income, the earnings from the investment could build in her hands practically tax-free.

So let's look at another option. Instead of Ron 'investing' the money and being subjected to tax on the interest earnings, let's have him loan the $100,000 to Carol. Now Carol can invest the money at 10% and declare it as her income and pay the tax (if any) on it. You are asking, but what about the Rules of Attribution and you are right. However if an actual legal loan agreement (promissory note) is drawn up and executed within the CRA guidelines, the Taxman will not attribute the interest earnings to Ron and demand he pay the tax on it.

By the way, this money can be 'loaned' to other family members in the same way so it is another effective way to provide investment income in the name of a son or daughter, while keeping total taxes as low as possible. This feature can also be used as part of an Estate Planning strategy to efficiently mobilize assets for the benefit of 'non-arms length' relatives. Once again we suggest you talk to your financial planner to learn how this could apply to you.

How can it be done?

It is vital that the right structure be used and there is a legal way. Three basic steps can accomplish it.

1. Have your lawyer, notary public, accountant or financial planner assist you in preparing the correct legal document for such a loan.
2. There must be a rate of interest clearly declared in the loan agreement and this can not be changed for the life of the loan (However the loan agreement can be replaced at any time with a new one if both parties agree.) Just remember that there has

to be proper documentation at each step of the way. When general interest rates are low is a good time to draw up such an agreement, for the interest rate in effect at the time of the agreement will remain in effect for the life of the document. For this strategy to get the Taxman's blessing, you must charge, at least, the current 'prescribed' interest rate which the CRA shows on their website as the interest rate for family income splitting loans. Using that rate will definitely not give the Taxman any room to come back on you.

3. The interest stated in the agreement must be paid to the lender. This can not be stated too emphatically. This loan interest repayment will slightly affect the taxes of the lender but we believe that you are investing the money at a rate that is far in excess of the rate in this loan agreement. Remember the interest in this agreement must be paid to the lender by January 30 of the following year with **NO EXCEPTIONS**. Failure to do this will cause CRA to attribute the whole of the investment earnings to the lender and you have not gained a penny. Our suggestion is that the borrower, write an actual cheque payable to the lender each year, (which must be cashed) so there is no room for CRA to question that the transaction was completed.

NOTE: Be sure that the cash flow of the borrowing spouse or child is great enough to pay the interest on the loan.

Okay, we have explained the basic advantages and shown you how to structure such an arrangement, and but we also want to point out some added benefits.

1. Ron has loaned Carol $100,000 at the CRA rate of 4%, but Carol has invested carefully and is earning 10%. This means that Carol earns $10,000 each year, but from that she has to pay Ron the $4,000 interest payment. Ron must pay tax on this $4,000 but that is better than earning the full $10,000 and

paying the tax on all of it. Carol is still $6,000 ahead and, at her tax rate, the Taxman is crying, so they have essentially split some of the investment income.

2. In addition, the interest on the money Carol borrowed from Ron (which is paid to him each year) is actually an investment expense on the part of Carol and can be used as such on her tax return. This will further reduce the tax she may have to pay

3. If the loan agreement interest rate was initially set at say 4%, but CRA drops their prescribed rate to 1%, which is what happened April 1, 2009, you can simply terminate the old agreement and create a new one with the new interest rate. The sweet part of this is that you do not have to change the interest rate in the promissory note should the rate go up. The rate is locked in for the life of the agreement. So now is a fantastic time to implement this strategy. You can arrange for an individual to have all the related investment income be taxed at the lower-income-earning family member's tax rate indefinitely.

4. The strategy is repeatable. If the higher earning spouse accumulates additional financial resources (e.g. an inheritance, beneficiary of an insurance policy, bonus) other promissory notes can be created to split income on the investment income from the financial windfall.

5. The "life of the agreement" is the final added benefit. You can make the agreement for the life of the parties or more precisely "forgivable on death'. So essentially it need not ever be paid back.

At the time of the writing of this chapter the interest rate for family loans as shown on the CRA website is the lowest they have ever been. Meet with your financial planner today to see if there may be a way to restructure your investments to take advantage of splitting income with family members.

SECRET 13

Giving Gives Back to You

> **" If you can't feed a hundred people, then just feed one."**
>
> - Mother Teresa

Most of us received our first introduction to charitable giving through our attendance in Sunday School and church. Each week we received some coins from our parents, to put into the offering. We so often wanted to keep them for ourselves because early on we had learned that these coins could also provide us with candy or something else equally as good. We may have even tried to secret them away from time to time, but the Sunday School teacher always seemed to know who had received a quarter and would quiz us until we could actually "find" that "lost" offering quarter. Although this little exercise did teach us to give money to the church it did not accurately instruct us on the benefits of charitable giving. As already stated we knew that money could buy us candy. This "purchase" in church only got us another hour of boring time in church. How much more effective this lesson in charitable giving could have been if we could have actually seen some direct result of our giving, such as a visit to a homeless shelter, or some needy children or similar.

An analysis of giving in Canada and the United States shows that 25.4% of the tax filers in Canada donate to a church or charity while in the USA it is only slightly higher at 30.4%. You may argue that periodically you leave a bag of old clothing for charities that will pick them up, but we question if that could really be considered charitable giving or simply getting rid of something you no longer want. The Bible, Koran, and other religious books, talk about charitable giving in many places, with the Bible suggesting that 10% is a good figure. I am sure I will get an argument stating that you are already having a hard time keeping up with your bills and don't see how you will ever get ahead if you give away 10%. However, there is an unwritten principle in the universe that shows that often, when giving is properly exercised, a person lives better on the 90% remaining than they had when they kept 100%. No one can prove this for sure, but regular systematic givers will attest to this.

In addition, our government, in their efforts to encourage charitable giving, has structured the Tax Act to provide a nice incentive to give. **TAX-CREDITS** are available to those who give, and although they are not as good as **TAX-FREE** situations they are almost as good. Here is how they work.

Direct Donations – When you make a donation, of the first $200 you donate you can receive a federal tax-credit of 16%. In other words, you donate $200 but on your tax return you basically say you donated $232. Because the provincial tax you have to pay is always a percentage of the Federal tax calculated, this credit reduces your provincial tax as well, so in actuality it now becomes closer to 26%. That is on the first $200 of donations. When you increase your donations beyond the first $200 calculation, your Federal tax credit becomes 29% instead of 16%, so your total donation essentially costs you just over $.50 for every $1.00 that you donate. To me this is an indirect way to get the government to donate to a cause you really believe in. Think about it.

Since most annual donations are less than $1,000, there are a couple of ways to get the best use of these tax credits. First, always make your donations under the same name and use the name of the spouse with the highest tax rate. This is not crucial for the name on the donation receipt does not have to be the person making the claim, however only one claim can be made per receipt. To keep things simple for Revenue Canada we recommend using only the one name, then have the highest rated individual make the claim. This provides the best use of the tax credit.

Let's look at an illustration to help us understand better. If both you and your spouse donate to your selected charities an equal amount of $1,000 a year, and your tax rates are 25% and 40% respectively, here is how your charitable tax credits will work out.

On the first $200 you will both be able to declare a tax credit amount of $232 plus the resulting provincial tax saving, so that equals about $258. On the remaining $800 actually donated, the tax credit and savings would be about $384 or about 48%. This gives an individual total tax credit for each of you in the amount of $1,642. Because the actual amount of the donation was only $1,000, your tax saving on the $642 tax credit difference was $160.50 ($642 times 25%) and $256.80 ($642 times 40%) respectively. This means that although together you donated $2,000 to a charity, you also paid $417.30 less in tax. In essence the government donated $417.30 to that charity. However, if the full $2,000 donation had all been done in the name of the spouse with the highest tax rate here is how the numbers would work out. The tax credit and saving on the first $200 would still be $258, but the tax credit on the remaining $1,800 would be $864. The combined tax credit used on your tax return would be

$2,922. The difference of course is $1,380. However, because of the rate of the higher taxpayer (40%) the tax saving is $552.00.

So with a little planning you can save an additional $134.70 in taxes. Simple, but effective.

The tax laws put a limit on tax-credits for donations up to 75% of your declared income, however, they do permit you to carry forward, for a period of 5 years, any donations not used. This ruling could give you another advantage as well. If your donations are relatively small each year you may want to let them accumulate to a year when you know you are going to have a higher income, or just to get the maximum benefit possible at some point.

Life Insurance Gift – There is another way in which you can donate to your charity other than by direct cash donations – it is a life insurance gift. It works as simply as it sounds. You take out a life insurance policy with the charity as the beneficiary and the tax department permits you to claim the premiums as a charitable donation. Then upon your passing the charity gets the full proceeds of the policy. A very simple and clean way to give a sizeable donation to your favorite charity and yet have some tax savings now.

Charitable Remainder Trust – If you want to leave a portion of your estate to a charity, why not structure it a little differently now, so that you can use the tax credits on your current tax returns, rather than having them apply in a lump sum to your estate? This procedure is a little more complicated but can have major tax benefits, now. The program is called a **Charitable Remainder Trus**t and needs to be set up with the help of a professional. Usually the charity you donate to has someone who works with them or within their organization who knows how to structure such a donation. Here is how it works. You (the settler) place your assets (whether cash or physical property) into a special fund which is administered by a trustee. The trustee oversees and operates the trust according to the directions recorded at the time of its establishment. The beneficiary of the trust (the organization that will get the funds) receives portions of the assets as directed by the agreement and upon the settler's passing away receives the balance remaining in the trust. However, while you are still alive the trustee continues to distribute funds to you as predetermined in the agreement. The nice thing about this arrangement is that Revenue Canada views the assets put into the trust as a charitable donation at the time the trust is established and depending upon how the trust arrangement is setup, will permit these donations to be subject to all the rules on charitable donations. As already stated, because of the complexity of taking such a step, a professional with intimate knowledge of these things must be involved and can show you the tax and other benefits that you can receive now rather than waiting until your estate deals with it.

The advantages are clear:

> You benefit immediately because you apply the donation to your tax return, whether current or over the next 5 years.

> Your income from these assets need not change, for the trustee will continue to pay you the amount agreed upon.

> Your estate saves probate fees because the assets flow directly into the hands of the charity.

> The charity knows what resources are coming its way and need not fear that you might not leave them in your will.

Finally we want to tell you about one more way to donate.

Donation of Property – Secret 6 told you about capital gains and the advantages of increasing your income using capital gains. Now we want to look at it from a slightly different perspective. Let's say that your income from all sources is more than enough and that you wish to take a previous investment and donate it to a charity. If that investment was one that was subject to capital gains, taking it into your own hands would trigger the capital gains tax. However if you donate it directly to your chosen charity, without taking it into your income, there are zero dollars in capital gains assessed. However, you still have the advantage of claiming the total value of the donation on your tax return and you now know how that works from the information provided earlier in this Secret.

Of course, the government has some guidelines as to what kind of property can or cannot qualify, but using this method of donating could save you some serious tax. Let's look at a possible scenario. Our illustration shows that you purchased $10,000.00 worth of stock 5 years ago. It was a good investment and is now worth $20,000. If you chose to liquidate that investment you would receive the $10,000 back without any tax liabilities but the $10,000 that you gained would be subject to the capital gains tax on $5,000. At a tax rate of 50%, this would mean that you would have to pay $2,500 in tax. Now look what happens if you give this to a charity. Your whole $20,000 value given to a charity can be declared with the resulting tax credits. Including the reduction in provincial taxes payable, the result is the same as making a donation of nearly $30,000. That is a tax saving of about $10,000 plus the $2,500 capital gains tax that you do not have to pay.

If your other investments are providing you with more than enough income right now and you will not have need of the income from this investment, why not make the donation while you are living. Take the tax saving against your other income, and you can still watch you donation do some good in the world. You can always provide this action in your estate to minimize the tax liabilities there when you are sure that you will not be needing the income from these investments.

The Bible records that Jesus made this statement – "If you give, you will receive. Your gift will return to you in full measure, pressed down, shaken together to make room for more, and running over. Whatever measure you use in giving – large or small – it will be used to measure what is given back to you." This is not a reason for giving but is a universally accepted rule of giving.

If you want to support a charity, remember the tax credits you get for doing it means that essentially the government is adding just under $.50 to every dollar you contribute. What a nice way to get the government to participate in your charity without getting directly involved.

At the beginning of the chapter we showed you that nearly 75% of the people in Canada do not donate to a charity. We believe it is because they feel the government is taking care of some of their social obligations for them, but as usual with the government, do you like the choices they are making with your money? Take back control and review your giving today.

> " A good exercise for the heart is to bend down and help another up."
>
> - Anonymous

14

Tax Breaks From Flow-Through Shares

When talking about investments, I remember my father stating that a great way to lose money was by investing in the stock market. His stated opinion was that you should "not invest any more than you were willing to lose". This opinion did not come from direct experience so much as from what he had heard about people who had "bet the farm" on some "sure" stock and seen it "tank" and lost everything. I think some of his opinion also came from the fact that the news media loves to over emphasize the scams and not the sound investments that can be made in some stocks. It is true, with the ups and downs of the stock market, direct investing is not for many people and I feel should be embarked upon only if you have a high tolerance for risk, and have become well-educated in the principles of stock market investing. But, it can offer some excellent opportunities to improve your tax and financial situation.

In addition to my father's opinion, you can tell from the earlier chapters of this book, I am always skeptical when the government suggests that we take certain action. However there are times that the government does come up with a plan to help certain sectors of the economy, that can be a great opportunity to save on taxes and earn income. This they did in a program called **Flow-Through Shares**. You may ask, can I lose money on it? Yes, just like you can on most investments, but the government minimizes the risk and permits you a nice tax saving at the same time. How does it work? Quite simply, really.

Because some sectors of the economy have different funding needs, and the government wants to see these sectors grow and develop, the government encourages people to assist sectors through investment. Let's look at a hypothetical situation. ABC Mining has done extensive research and testing of a piece of property that they own but because they have no revenue stream they cannot write-off these expenses. Therefore, the government permits this particular company to flow these deductions through to people who have invested in that company by buying shares. Let's continue with our illustration. All tests show that there are major deposits of copper not too far from the surface, but in order to get at these deposits a mine will have to be constructed and developed. To proceed with this development will require major amounts of capital before there is any hope of actually extracting the ore and selling it. In other words, capital needs to be invested long before there will be any revenue from the sale of the product. In fact, there may be considerable time between construction and when revenue is actually seen from the sales. This is where you as an investor can participate.

> **Flow-Through Shares**
  For easy numbers lets say that you earn $100,000 per year. If you invest $10,000 in ABC Mining you get a tax credit of $10,000. Which means that now the tax department considers your income to be only $90,000. So this means that your taxable income has been reduced by $10,000 for that year. If you were in the 40% tax bracket in the year you purchased the shares, the tax you need to remit is $4,000 less than if you had not purchased the shares. A nice saving, but it gets even better. These shares work differently than other investments because even though you purchased the shares for $10,000, when you sell, your adjusted cost base (ACB) is considered to be zero. So that means if 2 years later (typically you are

required to hold them for 18 to 24 months but some offers can be as short as 3 months) you sell them for what you originally paid for them ($10,000), that is the amount that will be considered to be your profit. Now the capital gains rulings apply so that half of the $10,000 is subject to tax. In the 40% tax bracket that means that you will have $2,000 in tax to pay. Even if the shares do not increase over the original purchase value you are still $2,000 ahead because of the tax savings.

> **Super Flow-Through Shares**

In October 2000 the federal government introduced an additional tax credit of 15% for most flow-through shares. For taxpayers in the highest tax bracket this 15% added to the 100% for regular flow-through shares became equal to a 137% credit. To top this off, several provinces give additional tax credits to the 15% offered by the federal government. They are as follows: Saskatchewan – 10%, Manitoba – 10%, Ontario – 5%, and British Columbia – 20%. Let's look in more detail at how these additional percentages could apply. If for example you live in BC, you will get an additional 20% tax credit. This means that as a BC resident, if you invest $10,000 in shares in a designated provincial mining company by the time you apply all of the tax credits, you are out of pocket only $5,060 of your own money for those shares. The balance of $4,940 has come from money that you would have had to pay the government in tax. Not bad when you consider that you still own the shares.

For a more detailed break down of the various provincial tax credits and how they apply to each tax bracket we suggest that you review the chart provided at

http://www.flow-throughshares.com/i/flowthroughbrochure.pdf

The risk? The risk is that not all exploration results in productive mines and/or sometimes shares can become worthless. Also, sometimes it takes much longer to bring the product to market than was expected and you have to wait for a long period for a return on your investment. There is also the fact that you cannot sell the shares for a period of 18 to 24 months as dictated in the share structure. The upside is, if your research into the investment was thorough and the mine does become productive, you could have valuable shares to sell or a nice income stream of dividend income for years to come.

Of course, if the shares increase in value you will be hit with capital gains tax on the sale of those shares, but if planned properly, that can occur when you are in a lower income situation and you still enjoy the tax saving now. Besides, remember, capital gains is one of the lowest taxed ways to earn investment income.

Let's recap. You purchase shares worth $10,000. Your actual cost for them is $5,060 and the government indirectly pays the remaining $4,940 (tax you would have had to pay the various governments). Some years later, when you sell, the shares are still worth $10,000. You pay capital gains on half of the $10,000 (approximately $2,000) and pocket the rest. In other words the shares actually cost you about $5,800 dollars of your own money and so you made yourself $3,200 profit.

If the commodities market does really well and the shares increase in value you could do even better, depending upon the final share price. We will not try to even project what could happen in that case.

Not bad for a program that the government created.

A nice secret to know for long term investing, but a little riskier.

"Take risks: if you win, you will be happy; if you lose, you will be wise."

Anonymous

" If you listen to your fears, you will die never knowing what a great person you might have been."

- Robert H. Schuller

SECRET 15

Consider the Offshore Option

We were very hesitant about giving this chapter a title like this, because of the bad rap that the term "offshore" has received as a result of money laundering and other negative press. However, if you are an international traveler, regularly wanting to escape Canada's harsh winters, or are just so fed-up with the tax system, this may be an option for you. We say "may be", because this method of tax relief is not for everyone. When we explain the procedure in detail to some people they lose interest because there are substantial up front costs involved and this action requires a major shift in the way one thinks about investing and accessing funds. We are not going to go into the specifics on this whole process but will give you an idea of what results can be created from this approach to your finances.

As we said, offshore investing does require a different way of thinking. Wouldn't you like to be able to run a company that does not have to report to anyone? Especially not the government, as to where or how the money was earned. No receipts or records of expenses need to be kept, and no report of how much was earned needs to be given to anyone other than those you want to know? Sound interesting? Then read on.

Such options are there, and can be very effective if structured correctly. Following is a list of some of the things that can be provided through such an organizing of your finances.

- Complete protection of these assets from spurious lawsuits or frivolous actions such as a messy divorce.

- An easy transition of ownership of all assets in the event of a death, without inheritance taxes, no legal hoops to jump through, no possibility of probate, and the opportunity to continue all aspects of the investments without change.

- An easy transition of ownership of any portion of the assets should you want to pass some of them along before your demise.

- **NO TAXES** of any kind on anything within that corporation.

- No need to give the government a summary or explanation of any part of the corporation.

- An opportunity to participate in investments that provide far better returns than anything found in Canada.

- No taxes on any money that these investments earn.

See what I mean by a major shift in thinking? How is it possible and how can it be done?

STEP ONE: Do some thorough research into this approach to investing. Learn all you can about what is involved and how it can be done from as many resources as possible. This course of action is not to be taken lightly. It is also crucial that your goals in Secret # 1 are well-defined and fit within these parameters.

Perhaps after reading this chapter you are going to want to go back and revise those goals.

STEP TWO: Find an organization that can do this for you. We suggest that you exercise extreme caution in making this decision because there are many unscrupulous operators out there, wanting to help you part with your money. The most logical way to find such an organization is by word of mouth. If you know of someone you believe has structured some of their finances in off-shore investments, talk to them. They will be able to tell you the pros and cons of such a structure and whether they are pleased with the organization they are dealing with. **Vital in this decision, is that the organization know how to do this legally and that it is structured correctly**. That last sentence can not be stressed too much.

STEP THREE: Properly set up the international business corporation. In this step we recommend that you discuss in detail with the organization that is assisting you, which jurisdiction (country) would be best for you. Facts that should be covered in this discussion are: how you wish to use the resources in the corporation, where you most frequently holiday, and the general lifestyle you anticipate over the next years.

STEP FOUR: The transfer and movement of the funds you wish to invest outside of the country, to this corporation. Again, because you want everything done within the letter of the law, so that Revenue Canada has no reason to take a closer look, you want to be assured that the organization you are working with knows what they are doing.

Once these steps are completed correctly, there should be freedom to invest as you choose without any reporting or taxes to pay. Yes, it can be done!

Many people ask if such structures are legal. We can say a definite "yes" … if they are done right. Are you sure they are legal, you may ask again? We respond by suggesting that you research and "learn about" Canada Steamship Line (CSL) for that is how that company operates. Don't know who CSL is? CSL is a foreign (offshore) corporation run by the children of our former finance, and later prime minister, Paul Martin. The reason we say "children" is because when he took public office he placed the shares he owns in the company into a "blind trust" and was not to be involved in the making of any business decisions of the company. (Right! We wonder what the conversation was like around the dinner table when the family gathered for special occasions.) CSL has been operating as an offshore corporation for years. The part that really galled us about that, was that when he became finance minister, the tax department sought to put restrictions on the flow of money to other jurisdictions, reportedly in the name of "money laundering". Of course, this was long after CSL had been setup in Panama and the rules would not apply to them.

Now you probably have more questions than ever. Over the years we have sought to answer these for people, so do not hesitate to contact us and we will arrange a time when we can address your options more directly and more discreetly.

Offshore is an Option!

> " Where will you be, and what will you be doing 10 years from now, if you keep doing what you are doing now?."
>
> - Napoleon Hill & W. Clement Stone

Tips that do not quite qualify as

Tip # 1: Did you know that if your spouse spent a number of years away from the work force and therefore was not making regular contributions to the Canada Pension Plan, that they can make a lump sum contribution in a later year? This will increase the amount of CPP that they will be eligible to receive when they retire. Talk to your accountant or tax preparer about this and see if it would be to your advantage.

Tip # 2: Did you know that if you moved at least 40 kilometres to start a new job or business, that you can deduct most of the expenses of that move? Visit the Revenue Canada website at **www.cra-arc.gc.ca/tax/individuals** and search under "moving" to get a list of the expenses that are allowed.

Tip # 3: Did you know that your medical expenses must exceed $1,844 or 3% of your net income to be claimed as a tax credit? Quite likely you are responding "mine are not nearly that high". However, you can claim for any 12 month period, so note the dates when tallying and use a period of time that will give you the highest total. Also, if you are paying any fees through work for health care coverage these can be added into the total. Like charitable donations it is also possible to combine the medical receipts under one taxpayer.

Tip # 4: Did you know that all child care expenses can be claimed within the limits of the tax act even if it is a neighbour or relative that is looking after the child? If you are making a payment for child care and getting a receipt for it, you can claim it, even if it is not a registered child care facility.

Tip # 5: Did you know that if your household income is less than $35,000 per year and you have small children at home, you can qualify for the Canada Tax Benefit? This will provide you with $1,228 annually for each child plus an additional $86 for the third or more children. Also check into the Canada Learning Bond which gives you $500 for each child born and $100 per year in grant money for the next 15 years. All children under 6 years of age also receive the Universal Child Care Benefit of $100 per month regardless of the family income, but this money is taxable in the income of the lowest income spouse. Visit the website at **www.universalchildcare.ca**

Tip # 6: Did you know there is a $65 per month textbook tax credit and that some of student's tuition and education credits can be transferred to you? Keep all of their receipts and ask your tax preparer how to apply them.

Tip # 7: Did you know that if you use public transit passes for at least one month, you can claim up to $100 worth as a tax credit?

Tip # 8: Did you know that effective the fall of 2009, grants of up to $250 per month for low income families and $100 per month for middle income families will be available for student's enrolled full time, in qualifying higher education colleges?

Tip # 9: Did you know that if you live in an area in Canada designated as a Northern Zone for a period of not less than six months, that you can claim a basic residents deduction of not less than $7.50 per day and maybe as much as $15.00 per day? You can also deduct 2 trips out of the Northern Zone for you and your family, and all trips that are for medical purposes.

Tip # 10: Did you know there is a very simple way to pay less tax? It is simply spend less. That's right, the less you spend, the less tax you end up paying to the government in GST and PST. We know a person usually only thinks of income tax, but these sales taxes can really add up. In addition, you will probably end up with more money to invest, so you really win.

> **"Problems are those things we see when we take our eyes off the goal."**
>
> Author Unknown

> **"You make the world a better place by making yourself a better person."**
>
> Scott Sorrell, speaker, trainer, coach

Conclusion

Okay, now that you have read the "secrets" you are quite likely saying to yourself those aren't secrets. Anyone who has looked at the Tax Code could discover them, and you are quite right. But which ones did you **NOT KNOW** about? Those were a "Secret" to you until you read this book. And would you have looked at the tax code, or would you have asked your financial planner about any of these, or would your financial planner have volunteered the information about them? Quite likely not. Now that you have read them, what are you going to do about them?

Let me tell you probably the biggest secret of all. Well over 90% of you are going to read this book and make some very minor, if any changes to your financial plans. Not because the changes aren't needed, but because too few people bother to take action. However, now you have additional information and there should be no excuse for not improving your financial situation. Unfortunately, no action on your part is just going to leave you with a feeling of guilt. Avoid that.

Take action NOW!

Begin by going back and reading that first Secret again and start with the simple actions suggested within it. Get some good books on goal setting and then go back through this book "secret by secret" until you have begun to or are ready to implement the secrets that apply to you.

> "Nobody can go back and start a new begining, but anyone can make a new ending."
>
> - Maria Robinson

RESOURCES

Books, websites and other materials we recommend for further reference.

BOOKS and ARTICLES

The Smith Manoeuvre
– Fraser Smith

ISBN 13: 9780973295207
www.smithman.net

The Impact and Cost of Taxation in Canada, The Case for Flat Tax Reform
– The Fraser Institute

www.fraserinstitute.org

Any and all books by
– David Bach such as,
  Smart Women Finish Rich

ISBN: 0385659679

Success Through a Positive Mental Attitude
– Naploeon Hill and W. Clement Stone

ISBN:0671743228

The Rules of Wealth
– Richard Templar

ISBN:0273710192

The Wealthy Barber
– David Chilton

ISBN:0773753184

Take Your Money and Run
– Alex Doulis

ISBN:0773762132

Success magazine
– one of the best subscriptions you can have.

www.successmagazine.com

Any and all, books and articles by
– **Og Mandino**

Any and all, books, articles or audio by
– **Zig Ziglar**

WEBSITES

Revenue Canada – (Canada Revenue Agency)
www.cra-arc.gc.ca

Canadian Taxpayer Federation
www.taxpayer.com

The Fraser Institute
www.fraserinstitute.org

Statistics Canada
www.statcan.ca

Canadian Tax Foundation
www.ctf.ca

Reference Desk – a source of information on the internet
www.refdesk.com

CATO Institute
www.cato.org

Office of the Auditor General of Canada
www.oag-bvg.gc.ca

Economic Freedom Network
www.freetheworld.com

We did not know where in the book to put this quote for it does not directly pertain to any of the information but it is so accurate we could not leave it out. Especially when we saw the source. Read it carefully and absorb its message for it is profound in its simplicity.

> " Be who you are and say what you feel because those who mind don't matter and those who matter don't mind."
>
> - Dr. Seuss

ORDER FORM

Liberty House Publishing
PH: 306-934-2192   FAX: 306-934-0484
EMAIL: libertyhouse@shaw.ca

The 15 Secrets The Taxman Doesn't Want You To Know!
ISBN: 978-1-897010-55-6
Cover Price $16.95

Volume Discount Order Form

Qty Breaks	Discount	Unit Price	Sub Total	S & H	Total	GST	Order Total	Charge Amount
1	0	16.95	16.95	5.00	21.95	1.10	23.05	
2	0	16.95	33.90	5.00	38.90	1.95	40.85	
3	0	16.95	50.85	7.00	57.85	2.89	60.74	
4	0	16.95	67.80	7.00	74.80	3.74	78.54	
5	0	16.95	84.75	8.00	92.75	4.64	97.39	
10	20%	13.56	135.60	12.00	147.60	7.38	154.98	
25	40%	10.17	254.25	20.00	274.25	13.71	287.96	
50	45%	9.32	466.00	25.00	491.00	24.55	515.55	
100	50%	8.48	848.00	FREE	848.00	42.40	890.40	

Visa _____   MC _____

Card Number: _____   Expiry:____/____

Name: _____

Company:_____

Address:_____

City: _____   Prov: _____   Postal Code: _____

Phone: _____   Fax: _____

Email: _____

Notes

Notes

Notes

Notes

About the Author

Dwayne Daku is a semi-retired businessman with a desire to share what he has learned about taxes during the twenty-years of running his own business. He is not an accountant or financial planner and does not claim to have the same knowledge. Daku just wants to share with the "average Joe" his understanding of what these professionals are trying to tell us. It is his desire that through careful planning, the basic information in this book will help reduce your tax bill.

How secret are the Secrets? They can be discovered by talking with your financial planner or visiting the CRA websites, but why spend the time researching when it has already been done for you in this book. Several accountants and financial planners have reviewed this information and agree with what Dwayne Daku is sharing.

Contact Information

E-mail: libertyhouse@shaw.ca

Fax: 306-934-0484